THE
SEX
CONTRACT

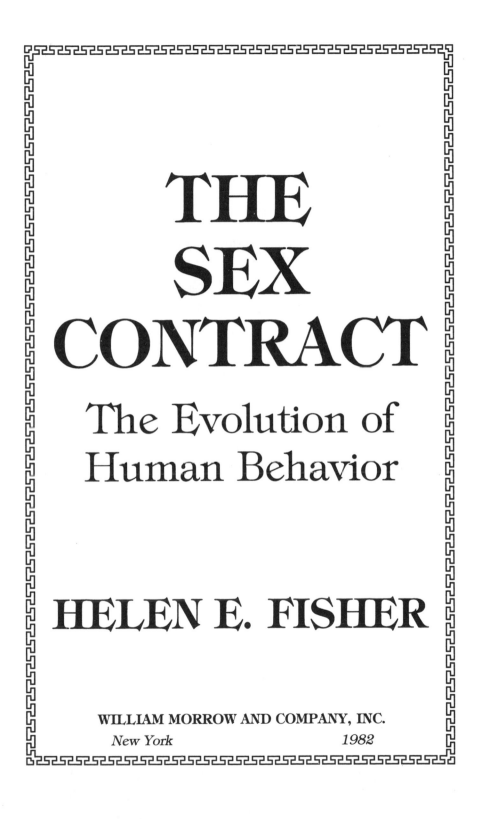

THE
SEX
CONTRACT

The Evolution of Human Behavior

HELEN E. FISHER

WILLIAM MORROW AND COMPANY, INC.

New York   1982

Grateful acknowledgment is extended to the following for permission to reproduce illustrations:

The American Museum of Natural History, New York, N.Y., for painting of early man by Z. Burian on pages 126–127 and for painting of burial site on pages 130–131.

National Geographic Society, Washington, D.C., for painting of *Dryopithecus* by Jay H. Matternes, © National Geographic Society, on pages 124–125.

Survival Anglia Ltd., New York, N.Y., for illustration of early hominids by Jay H. Matternes on pages 128–129.

Library of Congress Cataloging in Publication Data

Fisher, Helen E.
    The sex contract.

    Bibliography: p.
    Includes index.
    1. Sex. 2. Social evolution. 3. Human
evolution. I. Title.
GN281.4.F57   156'.5   81-11120
ISBN 0-688-00640-X   AACR2

Printed in the United States of America

First Edition

1 2 3 4 5 6 7 8 9 10

BOOK DESIGN BY MICHAEL MAUCERI

To my parents

FOREWORD

This book comes at a good time. The creationists and evolutionists are going after one another in public again. They have been at it more or less continuously for over one hundred years. For a while the argument made sense—science said one thing, scripture another and since there was not much evidence to go on, each side could use what little there was to support opposite conclusions.

It puzzles me, though, that the controversy is still going on, because today there is a lot more evidence, and *none* of it disproves an ultimate creation, and *all* of it supports the view that life today is a transformation of life in the past. The implication is awesome: *everything in the present is a rearrangement of things that have existed since the beginning!* Nothing new has entered the system; everything was there at the beginning in some other form. Surely there is both substance and splendor enough in this to permit each side at least to tolerate the other. Yet something more than understanding appears to be at stake—winning probably—for instead of listening to the harmony of change, partisans on both sides continue shouting slogans that have failed for decades to persuade anyone. Popular science personalities and state legislators especially appear among the last to accept what most everyone else takes for granted. I suspect that the argument is sustained only because both sides insist on continuing it.

So I think it is good that we review again the course of human evolution, good that we consider once more the old questions: Who are we? Where did we come from? Where are we headed? As we clamber to acquire the practical skills we need to earn a comfortable place of power and influence for ourselves as individuals, we are apt to forget the practical value our understanding of the past will have for future generations. This book is a story of human evolution; others viewing the same evidence would tell a different story—a change of emphasis here, a different connection there. But there is a fundamental difference between the way Helen Fisher interprets the evidence and the way the story is usually told. We are used to hearing it told by males, used to its consisting of unequal parts of aggression, hunting, male strength, male speed, female subordination, and children as burdens to be tended by women.

Helen Fisher takes another look and finds these aspects to be overemphasized in comparison with the extraordinary and somewhat neglected sexual changes one may infer females underwent early in the differentiation of our lineage. In her reconstruction she shows that changes in female sexuality were as crucial to human evolution as the adoption of erect posture and bipedal locomotion.

She tells her story clearly, using well placed verbal dioramas along the way, and offering a perspective that makes more complete an already extraordinarily interesting picture. The presentation will not resolve the creationist-evolutionist controversy—indeed it may add fuel for both sides to keep the fire going. But it will give others a more balanced and harmonious view of the important roles played by all—women, men, children—in the course of human evolution. In this representation we all play important roles and we are all involved in the process together.

—JACK KELSO
Professor of Anthropology
University of Colorado

ACKNOWLEDGMENTS

Thank you, Herbert Alexander, Ray Carroll, and Katie McAleenan, for your continual encouragement. Thank you, Eunice Riedel, for your invaluable editorial assistance.

I am also indebted to my friends Ned Barnard, Richard Berenson, Naomi Black, Stan Freed, Pieter Greeff, John Gurche, Michael Harner, Peeky Mathews, and John Pope for their contributions. Last, I wish to thank Jack Kelso and the other anthropologists at the University of Colorado for my graduate school training, my friends at the New York Academy of Sciences for extending my understanding of anthropology, and everyone at Reader's Digest General Books for my publishing experience.

CONTENTS

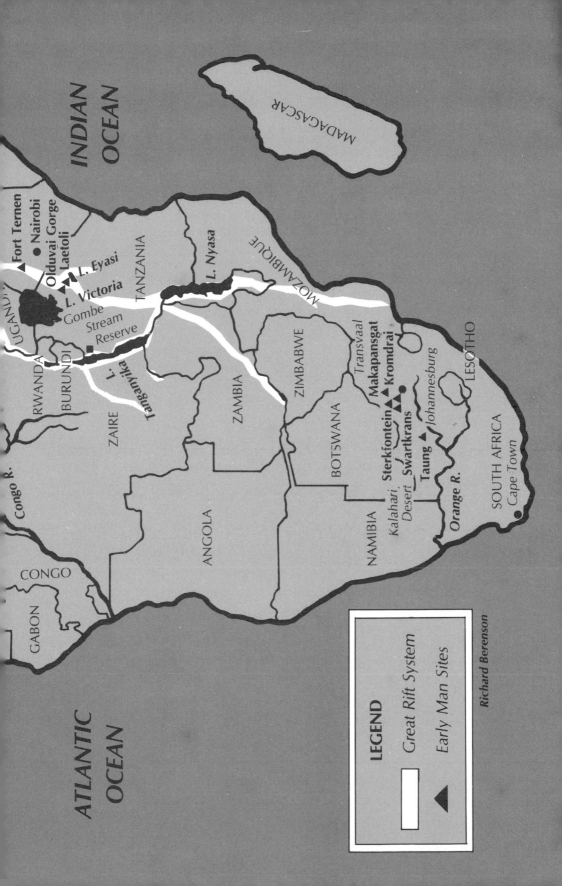

INDIAN OCEAN

MADAGASCAR

Fort Ternen
Nairobi
Olduvai Gorge
Laetoli
L. Eyasi
L. Victoria
Gombe Stream Reserve
UGANDA
TANZANIA
L. Nyasa
MOZAMBIQUE
RWANDA
BURUNDI
L. Tanganyika
ZAIRE
ZAMBIA
ZIMBABWE
BOTSWANA
Transvaal
Makapansgat
Kromdrai
Sterkfontein
Swartkrans
Taung
Johannesburg
LESOTHO
SOUTH AFRICA
Cape Town
Kalahari Desert
Orange R.
NAMIBIA
ANGOLA
CONGO
GABON
Congo R.
ATLANTIC OCEAN

LEGEND

Great Rift System

Early Man Sites

What a chimera then is man!
What a novelty! What a monster,
what a chaos, what a contradiction,
what a prodigy!
Judge of all things,
feeble worm of the earth,
depository of truth,
a sink of uncertainty and error,
the glory and shame of the universe.

—BLAISE PASCAL
Pensées

TO THE READER

Are you the richest man in America, the most powerful woman in business, the smartest kid in the class? Nature doesn't care. When Darwin used the term "survival of the fittest" he wasn't referring to your achievements or your endowments. He was counting your children. You may have flat feet, rotten teeth, and terrible eyesight, but if you have living children you are what nature calls "fit." You have passed your genes to the next generation and in terms of survival you have won.

This is the idea of natural selection that Darwin proposed in the *Origin of Species* in 1859. He also proposed a second, complementary concept—that of sexual selection. This is the mating game, the battle of who will mate and breed with whom. Every man and woman plays it. Who wins, who loses, determines which genes will reach the next generation and which will become an evolutionary dead end. So the game of love matters. So much, in fact, that it has influenced the entire course of human evolution and made us the remarkably sexy creatures we are today.

But why did we come down from the trees, evolve big breasts and penises, learn to bond and to raise families as "man and wife"? Why do human beings feel sexual guilt and jealousy? Why are we promiscuous? Why do we lie? Why do we smile? Why are we the only animals that cry tears? Why do human beings call someone aunt or cousin, fear incest, follow rules of whom to marry? Why do we endlessly recombine our squeaks and hisses, coos and grunts to make complicated words with complicated meanings? Why do we theorize about life, prepare for death, make love and war?

Anthropologists don't know how human sexual and social behavior evolved. All we have are clues. Many come from studying our closest relatives, the monkeys and the apes (chimps, gorillas, and orangutans). Others come from studying ourselves—human beings around the world today and our remains from yesteryear.

But there aren't many clues and assembling them is dangerous. Lay writers sometimes abuse what they know of this material to draw ridiculous conclusions about our past. Most scientists avoid extensive speculation for fear of being called hacks. And those few who enjoy working on the maze of human roots have almost entirely overlooked the role of sex—the spark that I believe ignited all of human social life.

So here is the story of human sex, our common human roots, and why we are the planet's most complicated beings. But first, a few words of explanation. Though the facts in this book are the product of years of technical research by many accomplished scientists—to whom I am very grateful—the hypothesis and synthesis are mine. They are the product of my Ph.D. dissertation and subsequent research. Because I am interested in bringing anthropology to the public, I have elected to write a book for a general audience. I have used relevant material from several disciplines, suggested a possible time sequence for man's development, and illustrated crucial points with reconstructions of early human life. I hope these theories stimulate your own ideas about our beginnings and why we do the things we do.

—H. E. F.

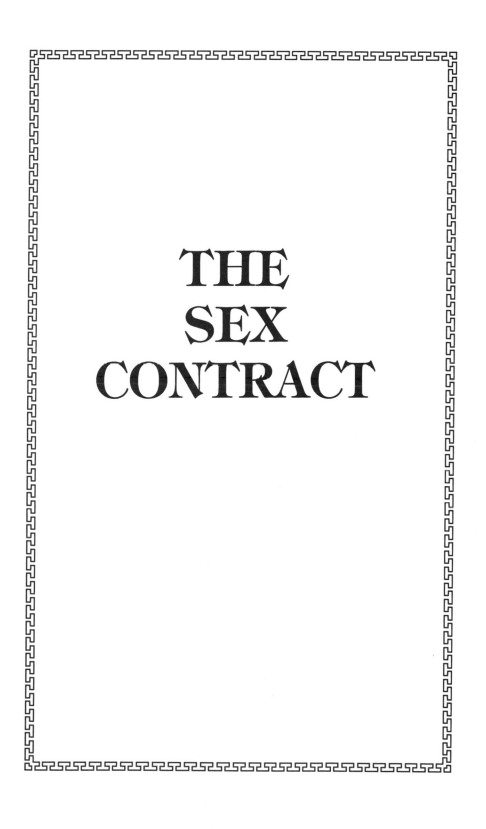

THE
SEX
CONTRACT

SEX
ATHLETES

O Western wind, when wilt thou blow
That the small rain down can rain?
Christ, that my love were in my arms
And I in my bed again!

—ANONYMOUS

American couples make love one to four times a week. This is low by human standards, say Clellan Ford and Frank Beach, the pioneering researchers on human sexual behavior, but when we are not actually making love we are often preparing for it. Men and women buy clothes to entice mates, cars to impress mates, meals to cajole mates—and advertisers know it. The morning newspaper features a leggy young girl, amid a cluster of suitors, in a dress every woman should own. Automobile ads show a dashing stud driving a car every man should buy. Deodorants, hair tonics, toothpastes, recipes, vitamins, exercise classes, sports clubs, aphrodisiacs, and thousands of other goods and services promise sex today.

We are surrounded by the mating calls of romantic novels. Movies and TV serials daily rehash love's problems. Country and western, opera, jazz, and rock and roll songs extol love's ecstasy. Drawings, photographs, and paintings depict love's pleasure. We laugh at sex jokes, play sex games, and exchange sex stories. We flirt with each other in the office. We parade for each other on the streets and we court each other at restaurants, bars, dance halls, and parties. We employ body stance, gait, gesture, apparel, vocal tone, and eye movements to court mates. And when we snare one, we spend time in bed each week making love.

The Cayapa Indians of western Ecuador are among the world's most sexually repressed people. The men spend much of their time drinking rum in tiny village shacks that border the Cayapas River. They are shy around women, whom they consider sexually aggressive. Occasionally an adventuresome man will go "night-crawling" to obtain a wife, but most men depend on arranged marriages to find their mates. Many have to be coerced into marriage. The Cayapa see the world as threatening and

21

cannibalistic. They refer to intercourse as the vagina devouring the penis, one of the many sexual fears that pervade daily life among these farmers and hunters. But, oddly enough, even here most men brag of having intercourse as often as twice a week.

Human beings around the world engage in sex regularly, and in many places people have created rituals to keep sex exciting. The Eskimos traditionally play a game called "douse-the-lights" to exchange sex partners. When the oil lamps are turned on again, gales of laughter and "I knew it was you" jokes add a touch of merriment to the long dark months of the Arctic winter.

On the balmy islands of Ulithi in the western Pacific, the Micronesian fishing people make love every day. Periodically they call a holiday known as *pi supuhui,* or "a hundred pettings." On this day or night individuals pair up and go into the woods to relax, picnic, and make love. Married couples cannot go together, and lovers are encouraged to pick a different partner. If the number of participants is unequal, a man or woman is shared. Even the children pick friends and play at hugging and caressing one another.

Among the Turu of Tanzania, most individuals have lovers. Marriage is a business for these planters and herdsmen, and though the women are taught from childhood to obey their husbands, they are not required to love them. Because the Turu feel it is difficult to preserve love with one's marriage partner, *Mbuya,* or "romantic love," is encouraged. Discretion, however, is essential. Lovers meet in the woods, exchange small gifts, and make love regularly. If they are caught, the man usually must pay a fine of sheep or cattle to the offended husband, but often the transgression is ignored.

These people enjoy a celebration of promiscuity at the circumcision rite of their fifteen-year-old boys. During the first day's activities couples perform a dance that imitates intercourse. Songs that refer to the penis, vagina, and copulation accompany the dance. The Turu say that if these dances are not "hot," or full of sexual passion, the celebration will be a failure. That evening they consummate what they have suggested all day.

Central India is the homeland of the Muria, a people who hunted, fished, and tilled the land centuries before the Aryans overran and settled this vast subcontinent. Today each Muria village has a *ghotul,* or "children's house," where the young go to live as soon as they are old enough to carry wood. In the *ghotul* all activities are shared, including sex. Each night girls and boys select bed companions and by midnight they are all settled down with their mates. Often a sixteen-year-old girl will cuddle a nine-year-old boy, or vice versa. Sometimes partners only hug and fall asleep but it is normal for the adolescents to make love. If a couple falls in love they are requested to sleep with others after three consecutive nights. "This is the way love is preserved," say the Muria, who believe that lovers should not permit their desires to burn out before marriage.

Along the headwaters of the Amazon the dense forests and cascading mountain streams provide food and water for the Jívaro Indians. Every man strives to have a large house a good walk from that of his neighbor, with as many wives in it as he can support. Unmarried Jívaro men steal constantly to the homes of potential wives, but married men often sneak about as well. Philandering is so common here that a jealous husband sometimes builds a *tampunci,* or "adulterer's trap," near the family garden. The trap is carefully designed so that when a lover appears along the path a bent tree branch will smack him in the groin. And though there are harsher retributions for adultery, the Jívaro continue to pursue their lovers.

In order to attract mates or paramours, people in every corner of the world have made extraordinary efforts to look sexy. African Bushmen women massage their infant daughters' genitals so that they will dangle enticingly by teenage, a mark of good looks to potential husbands. Ulithian women of the western Pacific tattoo the inner lips of their vulvas to enhance their beauty. Men and women have long tattooed their bodies, scarred their faces, filed their teeth, inserted lip-plugs in their mouths, stretched their earlobes, and pierced their ears or noses to achieve sex appeal. And where permanent body disfigurements have not been fashionable, people have donned every imaginable type of temporary decoration for sexual display. Among the most unusual are the two-foot-long penis sheaths made of orange-colored gourds that New Guinea tribesmen wear to decorate their genitals and the high-heeled shoes worn by Western women to accentuate their gait.

We are a species devoted to sex. We talk about it, joke about it, read about it, dress for it, and perform it regularly. We have legends to explain it, punishments to curb it, and rules to organize it. Everywhere there is an accepted way to court a mate, a proper way to marry, a legitimate reason for divorce. Sexual traditions and behaviors saturate our lives.

Why? Because the human female is capable of constant sexual arousal. She is physically able to make love every day of her adult life. She can copulate during pregnancy, and she can resume sexual activity shortly after having a child. She can make love whenever she pleases.

This is extraordinary. No females of any other sexually reproducing species make love with such frequency. All other females have a *period* of heat, or estrus, during which they copulate, and when they are not in heat they do not *regularly* engage in sex. For example, most mammals, such as deer, bighorn sheep, and sea lions, have a mating season. At this time the female comes into heat, and her sexual receptivity is broadcast to her suitors by changes in her odor and behavior. These signals touch off the courting ritual. The males of the species compete with each other and the winners mate with the females.

But once a female has conceived, her estrus ends. Her odor wanes, her behavior changes, and until her infant is weaned she will not come into heat again. She will have no physiological period of heat and thus no sex. The males of these mammalian species will have no sex either. They must wait until the females come into heat the following year before they copulate again.

Some members of the primate order also have a mating season. Lemurs, our small, agile, four-footed relatives who once roamed the trees of Africa, now live only on the island of Madagascar. Among the world's finest aerialists, they begin their day with airborne leaps from tree to tree in search of fruits and leaves which they devour in the presence of up to sixty comrades. Normally friendly, chatty creatures, they spend hours daily grooming each other's furry coats and playing with their young. Only in the mating season does this behavior change.

As the females come into heat, the males become aggressive and temperamental. They rush from one female to another, smearing them with fluid from their anal scent glands. Soon social life becomes an orgy of copulating lemurs. But the orgy ends quickly. In a few days the females conceive; their sexual behavior disappears; the chaos stops for another year.

Though our closer relatives, the monkeys and apes, copulate monthly rather than annually, their sexual behavior is also restricted. This was discovered in the 1920s at the Yerkes Regional Primate Research Center in Atlanta, Georgia. Here the Center's founder, William Yerkes, established that all of the female higher primates have monthly menstrual cycles similar to those of the human female. But, unlike the human female, they have a monthly period of heat that lasts about ten days and coincides with ovulation. Thus he concluded that the female higher primates enjoy sexual activity for about one third to one half of every month. That's a good deal more than lemurs, dogs, or cats, but it does not compare with the sexual abilities of the human female—who can copulate every single day of the month.

Since the 1960s more data has been collected on the sexual behavior of our cousins and it clearly confirms that human females are the sex athletes of the primate world. Characteristic of the monkey pattern is the sex life of the common baboon, and on the plains of Kenya where the squat, low-limbed acacia trees stand in clumps between miles of prairie grass, it is easy to observe.

A young female baboon has been in heat for about six days. To advertise it, the sex skin around her genitals has swollen with blood and blossoms below her tail like a huge pink flower. She has begun to exude a pungent, sexy odor. Days ago, when the swelling and scent began, five young males began to follow her around. To each she had presented her behind as an invitation to copulate, and each had leapt on her back and entered her several times. But now the female is fully ripe, and formidable contenders have arrived to bid for her sexual favors.

Among them is a leader of the troop, a top animal in the social hierarchy. He is a dominant male by virtue of his size and his ability to make friends. He sniffs the female, then suddenly turns on his male companions, rolls back his lips, yawns, and shows his fangs. His body is crouched and ready to lunge as he glares at his potential victims. It is a bluff, but the display works. His competitors back off nervously and the argument is settled. Then he jostles the female to the edge of the troop, periodically posing for his adversaries. Here he will

remain to copulate for as long as three days, stopping only to eat, sleep, or defend his prize. Between mountings the couple relaxes. She untangles his mane with her fingers, he licks her face and fur, and they nuzzle in friendship and camaraderie.

As her swelling declines, their "consort" relationship breaks up, and both male and female re-join the troop's daily life. If another female comes into heat and he can intimidate competitors, the male may have sex again soon. But his recent partner will not. For during their time together she has become pregnant. She will not have another estrus while carrying the embryo, nor until after weaning her infant. So she will have no suitors, or sex, for at least two years. Even then her love life will be brief. For a third of every month she will resume estrus, but soon she will be pregnant again and once more her estrus will disappear for years.

Like baboons, female chimpanzees also have a period of heat each month. And though it restricts their sex lives, they have learned to make the most of it. The most blatant example is the sexual behavior of a now-famous chimp named Flo.

Flo, who recently died of old age, was for years a member of a chimpanzee group that roamed a fifteen-mile home range in the forests and woodlands of the Gombe Stream Reserve, Tanzania. She was the pride of anthropologist Jane Goodall, who began a pioneering study of these remarkable animals in 1960. Mother of four and senior madame of the group, Flo eagerly serviced most of the males when she was in heat. As her bottom swelled and reddened, she presented it to the first male she saw and permitted him to pat, poke, and sniff her. Then she crouched as he mounted her from behind. When he was satisfied, she greeted another in the lengthening line of suitors who patiently waited their turn. Hours later she would relax in the forest underbrush with her most recent lover and permit him to groom her ruffled, sweaty hair.

During Flo's estrus she would copulate indiscriminantly with any male who wanted her. Among them she had friends, allies with whom she traveled in search of food and comrades near whom she nested at night. But she played no favorites. Only Flo's sons got no opportunity to make love to their mother.

Although Fagen, the oldest, was a young, powerful, and popular member of the group, he behaved like a child in her company and made no overtures for sex. Nor did she invite sex with him. Instead she felt compelled to mother him.

Flo's daughter, Fifi, watched. As a child, Fifi was annoyed when her mother began her amorous escapades. She felt ignored and often tried to wrestle the suitors from Flo's back. But as Fifi grew older she began to practice her mother's ways, tipping her buttocks to passing males in hopes of gaining their attention. Today Fifi has become what Jane Goodall calls a "chimpanzee nymphomaniac."

Yet even Fifi makes love only when she is in heat. For after a chimpanzee has ovulated, the pinkness of her estrus begins to disappear. Her swollen bottom shrivels and her odor becomes normal once again. Now her frenzied sex life is temporarily over. Though she may flaunt her genitals occasionally and even be mounted at times, until she comes into heat next month the males will be lining up for others. If she has become pregnant during her estrus, she will not ovulate again. During the first few months of pregnancy she will occasionally have a sexual swelling, but she will have no menstrual cycle, no regular estrus, no regular sex. And after she gives birth, a female chimpanzee will not resume her sex cycle until her child is weaned. For young mothers this is about two years. For fully mature females, such as Flo, the period of abstinence can be almost five years long. She eventually will resume her estrous cycle, but it will last only until she becomes pregnant again. So the amount of time a female chimp actually is willing and able to spend at sex is small—about 1 percent of her life.

Is the formidable-looking gorilla any sexier? George Schaller trekked through the dense tropical forests of Uganda and Zaire in 1959 to find out. Gorillas travel in small groups averaging about sixteen individuals. Each group has one dominant adult male who, by virtue of his silvery coat (which advertises his maturity) and huge size, leads a harem of females and defends their young. All year round they follow him, eating, sleeping, chattering, and grooming one another in his company. Younger, subordinate, black-backed males remain with their natal group if they have a possibility of running it some day. If not, they disappear to steal females from other groups and form their own harems.

Day after day Schaller followed their trails of discarded food, trampled vegetation, and dung, until finally a group of gorillas became used to him. And one morning Schaller saw some sex. A young female displayed her genitals to a subordinate black-backed male and he mounted her from behind. Then she mounted him and began thrusting until he turned and pulled her onto his lap. Schaller saw three rapid copulations within an hour. The commotion occurred within yards of the dominant silver-back, who appeared totally unconcerned by the ruckus. Schaller observed a similar sexual performance only one other time during his year of observation among the gorillas.

Because Schaller and other researchers found it difficult to find sexy gorillas in the wild, Ronald Nadler recently decided to explore their sex lives at the Yerkes Regional Primate Research Center. Every day he paired one of four female gorillas with one of nine males and recorded their behavior. The males never approached the females, and females who were not in heat rarely approached the males. But when a female was in heat—a brief period of about four days—she actually tracked the male and sometimes coerced him into copulating several times. One female began her sexual overture with a soft, high, fluttering speech as she backed her intended mate into the corner of the cage. When she had him pinned, she rubbed him rhythmically with her genitals until his penis grew hard and he penetrated her. Another approached her mate, grabbed him by the hair, rolled down onto her back, and pulled the male down on top of her to copulate face-to-face. In all cases the female was the aggressor.

Perhaps this lack of male initiative is because gorillas do not produce the obvious swollen genitals that serve to announce the advent of estrus among baboons and chimps. Whatever the reason, life seems to be a perpetual Sadie Hawkins Day for the caged gorilla—but only during those few days when the female is in heat.

Only our red-haired cousins, the orangutans, seem able to copulate all month long. These elusive creatures live in the forests of Borneo and Sumatra, where both males and females spend most of their lives alone. The orangutans split off from our ancestry about the same time the gorillas and chimpanzees did, and all three genera score in the same range on intelligence tests. But because the orangutans do not live in Africa, the long-thought cradle of mankind, and because they are semi-solitary creatures, investigators found them uninteresting. So until recently nothing has been known of their sex lives.

Nadler caged four orang couples at the Yerkes Center and watched. Every day he saw some sex. Each encounter began with a series of roars by the male as the female entered his cage. Then the male chased the unwilling and often frantic female around the cage until he wrestled her onto her back. When she succumbed, he spread her legs, held her thighs with his feet, and squatted over her to copulate face-to-face. During intercourse he often adjusted her position by turning her onto her stomach or side. Variations included sex while hanging from the ceiling of the cage, where she would suspend in hopes of eluding him. Neither partner grimaced nor expressed any pleasure vocally, as most primates do when they get sexually excited. In fact, the female often appeared bored by the whole procedure, looking around the cage, casually picking at her fur, and occasionally grabbing a bite of food—even during the height of the lovemaking.

When sex was over, the orangs retired to separate areas of the cage to clean up, and then the male often fell asleep. Occasionally a female tugged at her mate, slapped him, or pulled his hair to get his attention, but no male returned the gesture. The female was either ignored or rebuffed as he dozed off. Among orangs it is hardly a woman's world.

Although the female orangutan has no monthly sexual swelling, Nadler noticed that females were eager for sex only in the middle of their cycle. At this time the females spent more time grooming themselves. One female even bounced her genitals on a male's head as an invitation to make love. Some masturbated with a wire or by rubbing their genitals against the cage. The males also became more ardent lovers in the middle of the female's cycle, frequently demanding multiple copulations. From all this Nadler concluded that a trace of estrus still existed in the orangutan female, even though she can be coerced into making love all month long. Recently researchers living in the jungles of Borneo confirmed Nadler's conclusions. Females do copulate all month long. But generally they must be coerced and sometimes they are raped.

From this evidence, there is no doubt that the human female's sexual capacity far exceeds that of the apes. Though caged baboons and chimpanzees do copulate occasionally when they are not in heat, and wild chimps and orangutans are known to receive males when they are not in estrus, no female ape enthusiastically makes love every day of her monthly estrous cycle. Only rarely has a female ape been seen to accept a male while menstruating. No female ape initiates copulation as her fetus comes to term. And no female ape resumes her menstrual cycle to copulate on a regular basis before her child is weaned. Only the human female is different.

A human female's sexual behavior is not confined to the middle of her monthly cycle. Her genitals do not become engorged at ovulation. No all-pervading odor announces her ripeness. No heightened sex drive compels her to copulate at this time. A woman can make love when she is menstruating and she often encourages copulation throughout pregnancy. Theoretically, she can make love every day and every night, every month and every year of her adult life. In this respect she is unique among all other female creatures on earth. Women have lost their period of heat.

Actually, traces of estrus remain—and a few clever women use them for birth control. Shortly before ovulation, a slippery, smooth, colorless mucus appears along the walls and exterior of the previously dry vagina. Then after ovulation it suddenly becomes cloudy and sticky for a few days until it disappears altogether for another month.

Also at ovulation, the cervix, the muscular tissue that separates the vagina from the uterus, becomes soft and slippery. It opens and rises (perhaps to make more room for the penis) and then immediately after ovulation it lowers, hardens, dries, and the opening closes for another month. Some women feel cramping during ovulation at the moment the egg pops from the ovary to begin its descent into the uterus. A few women bleed slightly at this time. Others find their hair is unusually oily, their breasts are sensitive, or they have more energy than usual. The female's body temperature rises almost a full degree at ovulation and remains normal or above until the next menstruation. And she becomes more electrically charged as well.

So if a woman inspects the mucus in her vagina or her cervix daily, if she notes the cramps of ovulation, or faithfully takes her temperature every morning before rising, she will know when she is ovulating. Otherwise she will not. No period of heat—with its concomitant scent, swelling, and behavior—announces fertility. The result is "silent ovulation."

What a remarkable evolutionary twist this is. Because a woman has no obvious period of heat, a couple that wishes to have a child cannot tell when the woman is ready to conceive. So they must make love regularly. It is almost as if nature had wished human beings to make love daily, for in fact, the human female is particularly designed to do so.

It was not until the 1950s that investigators documented a second extraordinary human female endowment. Not only can she make love with impressive regularity (and has to if she wants a child) but her sex organs generate intense sexual pleasure—even more pleasure than the human male derives from intercourse. For nature has provided the human female with a clitoris, a bundle of nerves designed solely for sex. Even the slightest touch to this supersensitive gland causes sexual arousal. Furthermore, about four or five dense masses of veins and nerves congregate in the muscles of her genitals—and during intercourse these sensitive aggregates sharply distinguish her sexual performance from that of her mate.

As a woman becomes sexually excited, blood pours into the vessels of the genitals and the general pelvic area. The nerve bundles begin to expand. The muscles around the clitoris, vaginal opening, and the anus begin to swell with blood. This pressure is known as the "vaginal ache." Shortly, the spongy sacs that surround the vaginal opening expand to three times their normal size; the inner lips double their size, and the muscles of the entire genital area become engorged with blood.

Then suddenly the distended tissues revolt. They have become overwhelmed with blood and fluid. The pressure is too great, and they contract to expel it. First the wall of the uterus pulsates, followed quickly by the muscle of the outer third of the vagina, the sphincter of the rectum, and the tissues around the vaginal opening and clitoris. About every four fifths of a second a new contraction hurls blood from the pelvic area back into the general system. These rhythmic contractions constitute an orgasm.

For men, orgasm follows the same principle. Generalized physical arousal begins with a thought or touch and causes blood to flow into the penis, making it erect. The tissues of the penis fill with blood until the pressure becomes intense and then the blood-laden muscles contract.

But here men and women part company—the result of an extraordinary evolutionary change. At orgasm a man normally feels three or four major contractions followed by a few irregular minor ones, all localized in the genital area. Then sex is over. The blood totally diffuses, the penis goes limp, and the male must start from the beginning to achieve orgasm again. The female pattern is very different. She normally feels five to eight major contractions and then nine to fifteen minor ones, and they diffuse throughout the entire pelvic area. But for her, sex may have just begun. Unlike her mate, her genitals have not expelled all the blood, and if she knows how, she can climax again soon, and again and again if she wants to. In fact, the more orgasms a woman has, the more she can have, and the stronger they become. This phenomenon is known as "satiation-in-insatiation" and it sharply separates the sexual physiology of the human female from that of her male lover.

Some of the American women surveyed in *The Hite Report* confirm this. "One never is enough, two sometimes (rarely) is, but I usually 'need' about five once I have the first one," states one anonymous individual. "After the first orgasm I want to be aroused and have another almost right away. I am capable of several in one session . . ." wrote another, and a third said, "Each subsequent orgasm is stronger than the preceding."

Though these statements are not typical for American women, many of whom remain unaware of their sexual potential, all human females are physiologically capable of multiple orgasms. It just takes practice. As recently as 1966, not one man or woman among the inhabitants of a rural Irish island had ever heard of female orgasm. But sexual behavior in that region was severely repressed. The Polynesians of Mangaia Island know that female orgasm must be learned, and if one man does not successfully teach a young girl, her education is entrusted to another until she learns to climax several times.

Másters and Johnson first documented "multiple orgasm" in their revolutionary study on female sexuality in 1966, and they recorded another unique physiological attribute of the human female as well. This is the state of "continual orgasm" which they observed in some women. It is actually a series of orgasms that follow each other so rapidly that they are detectable only with machines. *The Hite Report* uncovered a few American women who experience this. Mangaian women call it "extended orgasm" and enjoy it regularly.

Almost all books on sex say that female orgasm is a uniquely human pleasure. Don't believe it. All of the female higher primates have a clitoris and some seem capable of intense sexual excitement. In a recent study, three rhesus monkeys were strapped to a table while a plastic penis was used to stimulate their genitals. Two of the three responded with vaginal spasms. In another lab test with stump-tailed monkeys, 143 sexual escapades were observed and intense body spasms and rectal contractions occurred in many females during the peak of intercourse. Flo, the notoriously sexy chimpanzee of the Gombe Stream Reserve, often copulated until she was torn and bleeding, a symptom of "satiation-in-insatiation." But these primates are restricted by their monthly cycle. Unlike the human female, they have orgasms (when they do) only while they are in heat.

Human females can have orgasms any time they want to. In fact, in the 1950s Kinsey reported that 90 percent of American women had their best sex at the end of their monthly cycle. This is a bit odd. It is not a time when a woman can get pregnant. Yet at this time blood pools naturally in the pelvic area—a phenomenon known as the "premenstrual tension syndrome"—and creates pressure in the female genitals that heightens the intensity of orgasm. It seems that nature has even made menstruation sexy for the human female.

Pregnancy and motherhood bring sexual rewards too. During pregnancy, new capillaries are built to feed the expanding pelvic area, and fluid congregates in the genitals—heightening the force of orgasm. Childbirth provides the genitals with added circulation too. So for a mother the contractions of orgasm are more intense than they are for a childless woman. And sex gets better with each new child.

Physiologically it is peculiar that human females experience orgasm at all. Only the male of the species needs contractions to pump his sperm into the vagina of the woman. Her egg drops naturally from the ovary into the uterus once a month at ovulation. She doesn't need orgasm to procreate. In fact, orgasm may be detrimental to conception, because the pulsations move downward starting from the uterus and tend to push semen out rather than up the vaginal canal. Despite this, orgasm can be intense and continual in the human female. Indeed, nature has outdone herself to make sex constantly gratifying for women.

Another female curiosity is the sexual world of the new mother. Almost immediately after the birth of her child the human female is back at sex again—and she can conceive too. In Western societies, where the bottle has replaced the teat for milk, mothers resume their menstrual cycle and begin to ovulate about six weeks after delivering a child. In other societies, such as that of the Kung Bushmen of the Kalahari Desert in Africa, nursing seems to suppress ovulation for about ten months. But unlike any other primates, human females can make love and reproduce years before their young are weaned.

It seems counterproductive that the human female is able to copulate within weeks or months after delivering a child. The human infant is totally helpless. Yet soon after parturition its mother's menstrual cycle will return; her sexual desire will reappear; she will begin to copulate again. And what if she conceives another child? Then she will have two helpless infants to support through the most vulnerable period of their lives.

This can create difficult social problems. Among the Yanamamo, belligerent warriors who live along the Orinoco River in Venezuela, a woman who bears a second child too soon after the first must often kill the newborn. When anthropologist Napoleon Chagnon lived among these people, Bahimi, the wife of a village leader, was forced to kill her newborn son so that Ariwari, her two-year-old, could drink her milk. Tearfully she reported to Chagnon that since she lacked enough milk to feed both youngsters, the infant had to be sacrificed to ensure the survival of her older son.

The Yanamamo practice a crude form of birth control. A pregnant woman simply requests a friend to jump on her stomach until the fetus is aborted. In other parts of the world women drink potions or carry amulets to prevent unwanted births. In a few places, cultural taboos dictate sexual abstinence after a child is born. Some Polynesian mothers insert a hibiscus root into the uterus to avoid pregnancy and women in industrial nations use plastic intra-uterine devices, birth control pills, diaphragms, and abortion to avoid having a second child immediately after delivering one. Close births are a uniquely human problem, the result of another evolutionary twist designed to enable the human female to engage in sex regularly.

As nature's final straw, she has endowed the human female with a few superficial sexual qualities of an unusual nature. Adult women around the world have breasts. These develop at puberty, like the fatty deposits on their buttocks, and both attributes universally distinguish them from men. At puberty human females also retain the high voice and hairless face and body they had as children.

Human breasts have no physiological function. They are subcutaneous deposits of fat around the teats and mammary glands that can be cumbersome to the bearer. They play no role in nursing. In fact, they can even smother the child. Fatty buttocks don't seem to have much use either. They do store fat, and among African Bushmen, where hunger may have been a problem, women have the biggest rear ends in the world. (These women's buttocks are, in fact, so large that a small child can ride on his mother's back, standing with his feet on her buttocks and his arms around her neck.) But fleshy buttocks appear on all women, from the cave-dwelling Tasaday of the Philippines to the disco dancers of Los Angeles, even though for most of these women malnutrition is no problem. Big breasts and buttocks appear superfluous, as does the female's high voice and hairless chin and chest.

Another superficially unnecessary female attribute is her ability to copulate face-to-face. Frontal copulation is not seen among the monkeys. It is unusual among chimpanzees, common among gorillas and orangutans, and the norm for human beings. In every human society studied, couples make love in this position regularly. Why? Because they can. The human female has evolved a vagina which is rotated forward—so for her it is comfortable to make love face-to-face. Furthermore, it can be intensely gratifying, because in this position her mate's pelvic bone rubs against her clitoris.

Irenaus Eibl-Eibesfeldt, a behaviorist at the Max Planck Institute for Behavioral Physiology in West Germany, has uncovered what he thinks is another innate sexual attribute—flirting. Recently he traveled around the world with a special camera which secretly takes pictures from the side. In this way he captured and recorded the unstaged flirtations of young women from Samoa, Papua, France, Japan, Africa, and South America. All flirted in exactly the same manner. First the woman smiled at her admirer and lifted her eyebrows in a swift, jerky movement. This briefly displayed more of her eyes until she turned her head sideways, looked away, and dropped her eyelids. Is flirting an innate sexual behavior pattern? If so, it is no different from the loss of estrus or the development of breasts—all unique human female sex gear.

So this is our legacy. Unlike all other female organisms, the human female has lost her period of heat. Thus she can make love every day of every month of every year. She can copulate while menstruating, pregnant, and shortly after she delivers a child. She can achieve multiple and continual orgasms, and the more she has, the more she can have and the stronger they become. They even increase with menstruation, pregnancy, and childbirth. She has breasts, protruding buttocks, a smooth body, a hairless chin, a high voice, and a forward-rotated vagina. Finally, she is a born flirt. All encourage sex.

Why has nature been so generous to women—and to men? The answer lies deep in the misty past—when our ancestors became sex athletes in order to survive.

BEFORE ADAM
AND EVE

He who thus considers things in their first growth and origin, whether a state or anything else, will obtain the clearest view of them.

—ARISTOTLE

Two hundred million years ago Africa lay in the center of a vast supercontinent, Pangea, which was surrounded by an even larger ocean, Panthalassa. Both land and sea rested—as they still do—on a layer of rock over forty miles thick, and below this crust of the earth's surface ran the restless molten currents of the inner earth. Soon these subterranean tides would tear Pangea into pieces and set adrift the continents we see today.

Pulled by the flow of liquid rock below, Africa was swept east some 180 million years ago, leaving North America and Europe behind. South America was drawn from Africa's western side about 50 million years later, and the south Atlantic Ocean appeared between the two. Finally, by 100 million years ago, India, Antarctica, and Australia departed from Africa's eastern side. Only Arabia remained attached to Africa 20 million years ago. Together they formed an island continent slightly to the south of their position today. To the west lay the Atlantic, to the east the Indian Ocean, and to the north the Tethys Sea (of which today's Mediterranean was a part), isolating them from Eurasia.

Africa itself had become roughly the shape it is today, but the jostling had left weak spots in its plate. And along two yawning gashes that stretched five thousand miles north through East Africa, the flat land began to gape and buckle. Where woods once reigned, now mountains began to rise. As these domes of rock broke the landscape, moatlike troughs appeared around their bases. For countless millennia, rubble collected in these depressions. Ancient seeds, leaves, trees, stones, and bones piled onto one another. Later, when these mountains became active volcanoes, lava sealed the ancient heaps. In these heaps, beneath layer upon layer of covering, lay the remains of life on earth as it had been 20 million years ago.

In search of early man, the renowned palaeontologist Louis S. B. Leakey and his wife, Mary, began to dig at a new site in 1945. The place was Rusinga Island, which lay in Lake Victoria, East Africa, in one of the ancient rubble-collecting troughs. Here the Leakeys uncovered a nearly complete skull of what they thought was a very primitive ape. Soon the skull acquired the name *Proconsul* after Consul, a popular English chimpanzee of the time, and made its debut in the scientific world.

Louis Leakey knew this skull lay somewhere in the lineage of ape and man, and for a while the newspapers featured the discovery. But *Proconsul* was too old, too primitive, and too apelike to be discussed for long. Besides, Leakey was interested in much younger fossils that looked more like human beings, and tantalizing specimens were in the offing at another site where his team dug yearly. *Proconsul* soon disappeared from scientific gossip.

Elsewhere, similar fossils had been found. The first had been uncovered in France in 1856, and in the decades that followed, reports of other finds trickled into scientific journals. The fossils were found at sites from Spain to China. Several hundred were unearthed in East Africa alone. Together they acquired the genus name *Dryopithecus*, or Oak Ape, after the dryads, or oak nymphs of Greek mythology. But they, too, were ignored in scientific circles, and by 1965 over six hundred specimens lay scattered in the museum basements of the world.

Then anthropologists David Pilbeam and Elwyn Simons gathered together all the *Dryopithecus* fossils they could acquire, casts of others, and pictures of more in an attempt to make order out of chaos. Each specimen dated between 18 million and 23 million years ago. Some looked vaguely like chimpanzees, others were similar to the gorillas, and a few Asian types were associated with the orangutans. None resembled man. But Simons and Pilbeam agreed that ape and man had evolved from the Dryopithecines.

Today there are over one thousand of these fossils, and every year new discoveries are announced. However, the sticky problems of our more recent ancestry have kept scientists at work on younger fossils, and *Dryopithecus* still remains overlooked. We know him by his bones, his surroundings, and the creatures that resemble him today, and from these slender clues his life can be reconstructed. This is essential to the story of human sex, because *Dryopithecus* is the creature from which we diverged to follow our winding road toward human life today. From him we inherited our eyesight, our general body type, our gregarious nature, and the fundamentals of our sexual and social life. So the story of the sex contract begins with him, when mountains rose through his jungle home of East Africa in the predawn of human history—before Adam and Eve.

Twenty million years ago warm breezes from the Indian Ocean swept westward onto the low flat land of East Africa. Here, broad rivers converged on a delta plain where tropical birds, marine fish, and whales foraged in the estuary. West of Kenya's sandy shores, mahogany trees, tropical evergreens, laurels, citrus trees, mango trees, and many others crowded the landscape, rising gently over the low continental divide of Uganda and spreading on to the Atlantic Ocean. Equatorial Africa was carpeted in green.

The temperature was slightly warmer than it is today, and the earth's heat pulled moisture from the trade winds almost every day. Often a cloudy morning turned into a wet afternoon as rain poured onto the steamy jungles, feeding the lakes and streams with fresh water and pelting the upper stories of the thick forest canopy. Here no seasons defined the ceaseless rounds of birth and death among the forest inhabitants.

As dawn shed light on a shallow lake, a hippo wallowed at the water's edge.* A flamingo hunting catfish stepped nimbly past a crocodile, who floated in a deceptive trancelike state. Two mammoths blew water on their backs to drive away the flies, as a nearby giraffe bent to take a drink. Beside them in the mud lay the tracks of several okapi and three rhinos which had stopped by earlier. A warthog, two tusked deer, a large pig, and an anteater would wander to the lake to drink as well. But eventually the land animals would return to the woods or to the tiny clearings among the trees in search of food and company.

---

*Like the hippo, most of the faunal and floral species mentioned in this and in subsequent sections are ancient varieties that are now extinct.

In the windless forest depths, butterflies danced in the dim light that filtered through the sky of leaves above. Golden moles plowed among the ground shrubs eating earthworms and insect larvae. Springhares burrowed in the soil, and cane rats, elephant shrews, hamsters, hedgehogs, and many other small creatures gathered nuts and berries on the damp forest floor.

Above them the trees rose as high as 120 feet. Each tree was encircled by tough vines which disappeared from sight in the interlacing branches of the first story. Among the leaves, orchids bloomed, flying squirrels glided from branch to branch, and bats hung in darkened crevices. Where the lower limbs entangled, the sturdy bough of a myrrh tree forked. Here an ancient relative of ours—Dryopithecus—lay sleeping in a nest of leaves.

Soon he rose on his hind legs, stretched to his full height of almost three feet, and swung his agile hairy frame onto a branch below. He crouched to sniff a flowering bromeliad that grew in a crotch of the tree. Its curved leaves had cupped water from yesterday's rain. After a thorough inspection he bent to take a drink.

Suddenly, hooting sounds broke the forest silence. Dryopithecus cocked his head to catch the sound. Friends were shouting of breakfast. He hooted back through the forest greenery, then quickly swung arm over arm along the branches of a well-worn path among the trees.

Less than a mile away he reached the scene of the commotion. Three younger males with whom he often traveled in search of food were shaking branches, jumping up and down, and screaming through the trees. He met each with a pat or tap on the hand and began to call too. The fig trees were in bloom and there were enough blossoms for all to eat.

Shortly the racket ended and he began to gorge, pulling the blossoms from the branches and stripping them of leaves and stems with his fingers and his teeth. He sought the biggest blooms, sometimes plucking one from below with his foot. Tailless creature that he was, he clung to an upper branch with one hand for balance and support, for as a child he had fallen out of the trees several times and he had learned to hold on well.

Other hungry Dryopithecines were hooting in the distance, and within minutes an older male appeared through the foliage, followed by two females with their young. Soon twenty animals had convened on the grove of figs. They all roamed the same territory between the lake and the dome of rock, and though they almost never defended their common ground, they traveled through it regularly, converging when food was plentiful and splitting up when it was scarce. Today they greeted each other with lip-smacking sounds, back pats, and hand taps, and promptly settled down in the fig trees to eat. Mothers fed their infants, but with this exception each animal gathered for itself. There was no thought, nor need, to share.

Within an hour, Dryopithecus finished eating and descended to a glade on the forest floor. Here the sunlight flooded through an open patch of trees. He stood on all fours, blinking for a moment. Others descended too, and a line formed behind a senior male, each animal grooming the one who sat before him.

His mother was with the group today. She lay basking in the sun until he roused her to pick the grubs from his back. She knew her son, who had drunk her milk and followed her through the trees for years. So she greeted him and settled down to clean his neck. Near them his younger sister played tag with a friend, racing around a fig tree and tickling her playmate when she caught him. Three friends were eating ants that wove their way like a military column through the group, while one young female playfully poked a hedgehog that entered the clearing. The morning passed uneventfully.

By midday, many began to feed again. Three newcomers arrived, and among them was a young female who timidly approached those who still remained on the ground. She was eager, but not for food. Immediately Dryopithecus rose to greet her. As he approached she turned away, looked at him over her shoulder, and tipped her buttocks toward his snout. She was in heat, and he could smell it. Soon they were intensely grooming one another, until he pulled her to her feet. Then she crouched before him on all fours and he mounted her from behind.

The mating did not go unnoticed, and soon the fig brigade

disbanded. Dryopithecus had ejaculated, and he was grooming the female when an older male elbowed his way through the growing crowd. The new suitor nudged Dryopithecus aside and began to inspect the female. But his amorous gestures ended abruptly. A shocking screech resounded through the clearing.

Dryopithecus wheeled around to face the sound. In a moment he saw a saber-toothed tiger leap into the glade and pounce on a young mother who stood on all fours before her infant with her teeth bared. Dryopithecus crouched and bared his own huge fangs to the intruder. Then he fled. He bolted into a fig tree without looking back, following others who hollered to each other as they vanished from the slaughter below.

The fig trees were a regular stopping place for the thirty or so individuals who roamed the territory near the lake. These trees, situated at the center of the area they ranged, provided a fine place to congregate when the fig flowers bloomed or the fruit ripened. But now the frightened group split up. Some headed for the wild pear trees, others for the cashew thicket, and some farther up the foothills below the mountain peak. They would see each other soon, probably tomorrow at the fig grove, but none would descend to the grassy glade to frolic on the ground.

As Dryopithecus rested in a rubber tree, he looked around to get his bearings. To the east was the lake, where he went occasionally to drink and to eat the lichi fruit that grew on the trees at the water's edge. To the west rose the dome of rock that marked the boundary of his range, and around him stretched the forest and the clearings he called home. Soon the sky grew dark and rain began to drip through the sodden leaves and down his neck. He hunched his shoulders, shielded his head with his hands, and squatted among the leaves.

The afternoon passed slowly. Twice he moved to the thorn trees to eat the tiny, honey-tasting flowers. Once he hooted through the branches to locate friends. The rest of the rainy day he dozed. He had no plans for tomorrow, no thoughts of yesterday, and though he remembered the incident with the saber-toothed tiger—and possibly missed the mother and infant left behind—his thoughts were not on life and death.

But today the young female had conceived his child. Within months she would bear the infant and suckle it with her breastless teats. When the baby got older she would show it where the turtles laid their eggs and how to catch young lizards; for years the infant would follow her through the trees, eating nuts, berries, and new leaves. If her tiny offspring fell from the trees, she would fetch him and defend him with her teeth if necessary, for she was as big and strong as Dryopithecus and did not need his help to raise the child. In fact, Dryopithecus's fatherly duties were nonexistent. Though he might play with the infant on the forest floor when all was safe, he would never recognize the child as his own.

As the sun sank behind the mountainside, day turned into evening, and after a supper of kiaat leaves, Dryopithecus began to make his nest. Carefully he folded branches into a leafy bed, lay down, and curled his knees toward his chest. He had lived another day, fathered a child, and passed his genes on to the next generation.

Soon in geologic time his world would change; from one of his many descendants would come the first ancestors of man.

Between 18 million and 17 million years ago the African/ Arabian plate of the earth's surface shifted to the north and slammed into Eurasia—first in the area of the Zagros and Taurus Mountains in the Middle East and shortly later in southern Spain. Land that had been pulled apart by the currents of the inner earth millions of years before had been reconnected.

With the shift of continents, the Tethys Sea was surrounded by land and became a huge lake—known today as the Mediterranean Sea. Soon the lake turned into a swamp and intermittently a dry woodland area where the plants and animals of Europe mingled with those of Africa.

Africa was no longer part of an island continent, for a vast land corridor now stretched through Arabia—connecting Africa to Eurasia. Once again the forests of the south met those to the north in a continuous belt of jungle that spread from South Africa to India. In these forests, varieties of Dryopithecines and other tree dwellers continued their daily rounds of eating and relaxing in their leafy universe above the ground. Rhinos and other hoofed grazers still ambled in small groups from glade to glade, to forage between the trees. Around them rabbits and moles followed their trails on the forest floor. Every morning the sun warmed the trees and clearings and every afternoon warm rain fed the streams and lakes.

But the warm, humid weather was not to last much longer. The Tethys Sea had been the earth's heating system, circulating tropical currents to the oceans of the world, and now it was trapped. Warm water no longer lapped the shores of the world's continents. The winds that had once sucked warm water from the seas now carried cooler moisture and dumped cooler rain on the tropical forests of the earth. In fact, since the dawn of the Cenozoic geological age—when mammals replaced the reptiles 65 million years ago—the world temperature had begun to fall. Now it dropped again; the earth was cooling down.

Further climatic complications struck East Africa. As the African continental plate slipped north, the two parallel rifts in the earth's surface that stretched through East Africa began to spread apart. Between them the ground sank and formed the landscape we know today—a series of low valleys nestled between mountainous highlands on either side. As a result, the eastern trade winds from the Indian Ocean expelled their moisture east of the mountains of the eastern rift and the western trade winds from the Atlantic and the Congo Basin dropped their moisture before rising over the western rift. The Rift Valley region of East Africa was in "rain shadow," as the highlands on all sides stole the moisture from the clouds. The land was drying up.

The mountains began to bubble over with molten rock. Some had begun to spout as early as 20 million years ago; but by 14 million years ago, Yelele, Moroto, Napak, Kadam, Elgon, Kisingiri, and Tinderet threw off steam, clouds of ash, and streams of lava on the plants and animals below.

With the cooling of the earth, the effects of rain shadow, and the active volcanoes in the region, the tropical forests of East Africa began to shrink—as the forests were shrinking around the world. The tropical evergreens and deciduous trees that once packed the land, intertwining to create a thick, multistoried canopy, began to disappear as two new ecological niches began to open up.

At the forest fringe woodlands appeared. These were areas in which single-storied trees stood far apart, barely touching each other with their boughs. Often these trees rose in clumps surrounded by boulevards of prairie grass. And where water was even more scarce, the woodlands yielded to a second botanical niche, the savannahs—miles and miles of prairie grass. Where formerly the grasses and herbs had struggled to survive below a sea of leaves, now they began to spread and dominate the landscape.

With the growth of the woodlands and savannahs, most of the ancient forest species died out. The animals that could adapt congregated in the open spaces to eat, to mate, and slowly to evolve into new forms.

Now the drenching downpours that had soaked the forests every afternoon were a thing of the past. Monsoons still swept off the Indian Ocean to dump water on East Africa between November and April, but during the rest of the year the tropical plants were dormant. The fig trees, acacia trees, and trees of the mango, wild pear, lute, and lichi families no longer bore their fruit or flowers all year long. And the tender shoots, new leaves and buds that had always appeared throughout the year grew only in the rainy season.

The lush, protective world of *Dryopithecus* was coming to an end and our first true ancestors would soon appear from among the trees.

THE PUZZLE
OF THE
MISSING LINK

"Give me a tooth and I'll reconstruct the animal."

—CUVIER

No single scientific topic so captivated or shocked so many people in the last century as did the subject of the "missing link." When, in the mid-1800s, Darwin announced that man had evolved from a lower form, the upper classes of England responded as those of continental Europe had when Copernicus declared that the earth revolved around the sun. They were horrified. The wife of the Bishop of Worcester summed up the calamity succinctly: "Descended from the apes! My dear, let us hope it is not so; but if it is, let us hope that it does not become generally known."

Well, the bishop's wife should not have been so worried. We are not descended from the apes. Instead, man and ape are both descended from the Dryopithecines—those tree-living fruit lovers who swung through the trees of Africa, Europe, and Asia 20 million years ago. But in Darwin's time no one knew this, so scientists began to search for the missing link between man and ape.

By the turn of the century French anthropologists had unearthed several specimens of ancient man on their own soil. The findings showed that modern man had lived about 23,000 years ago and produced spectacular cave art in southern France, and that a more ancient, beetle-browed variety of man had left behind handsome stone tools in French fields and caves about 70,000 years ago. The French delighted in reminding their English colleagues that they, at least, could trace their heritage to a distant and distinguished past.

But not for long. In 1912, British geologist Arthur Smith Woodward and an amateur archaeologist and lawyer named Charles Dawson announced their joint discovery of Dawn Man before the Geological Society of London. To prove it they displayed fragments of an ancient skull and jaw along with flint tools which they had found in a gravel pit at Piltdown in Sussex, England. The skull fragments looked like those of a man, the jaw like that of an ape. The missing link had been discovered, they claimed, and news of Dawn Man, or Piltdown Man, hit the papers like a bomb.

So began the largest scientific "whodunit" of our century. Many scientists were skeptical of the fossils at first, thinking that perhaps the bones of an ape had somehow become mixed with those of a man sometime in the geologic past. But the following year a young French priest, Pierre Teilhard de Chardin (who would later become a world-renowned theologian and palaeontologist), found an apish tooth in the same Piltdown gravel pit. Two years after that, Dawson found more manlike skull parts and an apelike tooth as well. They could not have found better pieces to support their view, for if the first fossils left some scientists dubious, the second and third discoveries confirmed that Piltdown Man had indeed sported a primitive, apelike jaw and an expanded human brain. Since Darwin's time scientists had argued over which came first, man's modern jaw or his enlarged brain, and the English—proud to have solved the riddle in their own backyard—gloated over their discovery.

But as the decades passed, fossils appeared in Africa that made Piltdown Man appear peculiar. And in 1953 a new chemical testing procedure revealed that the Piltdown fossils were all fakes. The skull parts were those of a modern man, the jaw fragments and teeth those of an orangutan. The bogus fossils, "worked" and stained to look antique, had been planted in the ground along with recently carved, ancient-looking tools.

No one knows who perpetrated this extraordinary hoax. Smith Woodward, a dedicated, gullible scientist, seems not to have been involved. He died thinking his theory held. The main suspect has been Dawson, a glory hound who may have had it in for academic types. He died suddenly in 1916—shortly after receiving great acclaim—and could not be interrogated. But accusations against other possible culprits still appear.

In 1980, Teilhard, who had died in 1955, was accused as a co-conspirator. He was the only one of the three alive at the time of the exposure and indeed he might have incriminated himself in the hoax. For in a letter of self-defense he had made a number of bad errors, among them a fatal slip in which he claimed to have seen the fossils two years before they were discovered. Another new suspect is one of Smith Woodward's colleagues who may have wished to humiliate him. All the suspects are dead now, however, and the Piltdown hoax is still a mystery. Nevertheless, Piltdown Man, as fraudulent as he has been proven, remains the "discovery" that popularized the concept of the missing link.

The uncovering of such an elaborate scientific fraud was sobering, and until 1961 no one ventured to proclaim his fossil specimens as the first true ancestor of man. That year, however, L. S. B. Leakey received a piece of bone that Fred Wicker had found weathering out of a hillside on his farm in Kenya. Leakey, a born and bred Kenyan who had been collecting artifacts since the age of twelve, had become a fossil hunter of world renown, and when he examined the bone he knew it belonged to an ancient primate.

As soon as the rainy season ended, he began excavation. Wicker's farm lay in the Rift Valley region of East Africa at the base of Mt. Tinderet—a volcanic cone that had spewed black clouds of ash on *Dryopithecus* millions of years before. But now trees, grasslands, and dry summer stream beds cut across the foothills below the dead volcanic peak.

Within weeks Leakey found two fragments of an upper jaw, an upper canine tooth, and a lower molar which were tested and dated 14 million years old.* The site was called Fort Ternan, the fragments christened *Kenyapithecus wickeri*—the Kenya Ape of Mr. Wicker. The following summer Leakey returned to find part of a lower jaw and more isolated teeth of the same type of creature he had named the year before. They were indeed all part of the long-sought missing link, but it was not Leakey who recognized the significance of his find.

Often in history great discoveries seem to occur in tandem, as when Wallace proposed the theory of selection by survival of the fittest while Darwin was writing his opus on the same subject. And, as if by fate, the same year that Leakey began to dig, Elwyn Simons, a palaeontologist then from Yale University, began restudying a fossil which had been in the Yale anthropology

---

*Starting between your two front teeth and counting toward the rear in one quadrant of your mouth, you can identify two flat incisor teeth, one slightly pointed canine tooth, two rounded, double-pointed pre-molar teeth, and finally three large, rounded molar teeth—the last being your wisdom tooth.

laboratory since 1932. This fragmentary part of an upper jaw had been recovered by a young Yale graduate student, G. Edward Lewis, who had roamed through the Siwalik Hills of India with a packhorse as his sole companion. In this dry, eroded region some one hundred miles north of New Delhi, ancient fossil beds lay exposed. There Lewis picked up perhaps the single most exciting clue to human evolution.

To Lewis the jaw piece looked strangely human because it lacked the protruding snout so characteristic of both primitive and modern apes. So for a species name he dubbed it *brevirostris*, Latin for short-snouted. For a genus name he called it *Ramapithecus*, or Rama's Ape, after a mythical prince in an Indian epic poem. He placed his fossil in the family Hominidae to emphasize its direct descent to man.

Lewis never published his dissertation on *Ramapithecus*, and for thirty years the piece of upper jaw lay in a box in the basement of his alma mater. But in 1961, as Leakey dug on Mr. Wicker's farm, Simons examined it and proclaimed it a protohominid—the first in the line toward man. Within months the announcement of Leakey's discovery reached Simons, and when he compared the fossils, Simons concluded that the specimens from both Africa and India represented the missing link.

Soon other fossil remnants of this short-snouted creature were found in Pakistan, Hungary, Greece, Turkey, and the basements of academic institutions. Eventually scientists came to call them all *Ramapithecus*—the name by which they were first properly identified in 1932 by the student G. E. Lewis. The Fort Ternan fossils that Leakey found in East Africa are the oldest, dating from between 14 million and 12.5 million years ago. The others span the time from 12 million to 8 million years. And for a while anthropologists—convinced that the missing link had finally been found—sat fingering these fossils, or replicas, and weaving tales about our beginning.

Now, once again, they are not so certain. For another messy complication has arisen and the intellectual battle lines are drawn. This time the questions stem not from phony or real bones, but from a biochemical discovery. It began in 1967 when Vincent Sarich and Allan Wilson disappeared into the chemistry lab at Berkeley to look at certain blood protein molecules. They knew that related species, like the grizzly and polar bear, would have similar blood proteins. So by measuring the look-alike qualities of human and other primate blood proteins they established that humans were most closely related to the African apes, the chimpanzee and gorilla. This was fine. Anthropologists all knew that. But their next ingenious conclusion brought down the sky.

Sarich and Wilson knew that the molecular structure of blood proteins evolved at a steady rate. They also knew when specific creatures like horses and zebras, or dogs and foxes, diverged from one another in the past. So, by comparing the proteins of these species whose ancestry they could pinpoint, they were able to conclude how fast these proteins evolved. Then they measured the amount of difference in blood protein molecules between modern man and the modern African apes. And, working backward, they established when man and ape diverged. Their answer: only 4 million to 6 million years ago. Sarich put it bluntly: "*Ramapithecus* cannot be a hominid, no matter what it looks like."

Palaeontologists panicked. Some said the biological "protein clock" kept lousy time, and they stuck by their beloved *Ramapithecus*. Others put these fossils away in basements and publicly renounced the view that *Ramapithecus* was part of our heritage at all. Some palaeontologists conceded that *Ramapithecus* may be only a close relative—not the missing link.

Regardless of the argument, *Ramapithecus* lived at the crucial time when our first relatives—the protohominids—must have been descending to the ground. And in some respects *Ramapithecus* resembles modern man. But whether he is our first ancestor or just a long-dead next of kin, he's all we've got, and his bones give anthropologists a few essential clues about the missing link.

But what can a few bits of ancient jaws and teeth—enough to fill one shoebox—say about the evolution of man, the planet's most complicated being? A lot. Here are the clues.

The reconstructed jaws of *Ramapithecus* are very different from those of their predecessors, the Dryopithecines. They are thicker in the area of the molar teeth. The lower jaw is buttressed with extra bone and the sides of the jaw (which connect it to the skull on either side) have a more human shape. The cheek teeth (molars and premolars) of *Ramapithecus* are large, the sides are steep, and the chewing surfaces are round and flat. Furthermore, these teeth are tightly packed together. Dryopithecine molars are longer from front to back, the chewing surfaces are sharper, and they are loosely spaced apart. An outstanding difference between these creatures is measured in the amount of enamel that coats their molar teeth. Dryopithecine molars have a thin coating of enamel, whereas those of the Ramapithecines are coated with thick crusts of this wear-resistant stuff.

As the back teeth were becoming larger in *Ramapithecus*, the front teeth were getting smaller. Unlike the long, daggerlike, interlocking canines that *Dryopithecus* displayed, those of *Ramapithecus* had become broader, rounder, less like fangs. The front teeth differed too. *Dryopithecus* had big bucked teeth, while *Ramapithecus* had smaller teeth set more vertically in his head. *Ramapithecus* was losing his muzzle too. Unlike the protruding snout of *Dryopithecus*, that of *Ramapithecus* was becoming flat like ours.

In short, the mouth of *Ramapithecus* had become sturdier, more durable, more efficiently designed to chew. While *Dryopithecus* had a projecting snout, shearing fangs and bucked front teeth that served to pluck, strip, husk, or shell the fleshy fruits and berries that were his fare, *Ramapithecus* had thick-enameled, rounded molars, small front teeth, and a buttressed jaw that swung below his skull to grind harder food. Clearly *Ramapithecus* had changed his diet by 10 million years ago.

The purpose of these dental features is confirmed when the teeth of *Ramapithecus* are compared with those of the gelada baboons. These relatives of the more common savannah baboons roam the high plateau country of Ethiopia today. They spend their lives squatting on the arid, grassy slopes of the ancient rift escarpments, eating tough seeds, roots, leaves, and blades of grass. All day long they pick up the tiny, relatively unnutritious morsels with their fingers and chew—grinding their molars from side to side to crush their food.

Like the molars of *Ramapithecus*, gelada molars are very large and tightly packed together; the chewing surfaces are round and flat; they have thick enamel coatings. Geladas also have reduced fangs, a short snout, and a relatively flat face—just like *Ramapithecus*. Unlike the Dryopithecines, our first ancestors evidently spent many of their waking hours chewing tough food.

Ramapithecus also had highly polished teeth, and from this clue the brand-new field of taphonomy has confirmed what *Ramapithecus* ate and where he ate it. This science examines the processes by which fossilized bones appear in certain quantities and configurations. The pioneering taphonomic study was done in 1967 among the Hottentots of South-West Africa (Namibia). Here a scientist watched these herdsmen butcher and eat their goats. What the Hottentots didn't eat, their dogs did, and the last remains were carried off by the local gerbil population. From a survey of the damages on the bones and from an examination of their final resting places, it became clear how the goats were butchered, who ate which parts in what fashion, and who tossed or dragged the remains to where. In this way taphonomy works backward, by acquiring present-day information and then applying it to the deposition and condition of ancient bones.

In 1979, Alan Walker, an anthropologist at Johns Hopkins University, applied the taphonomic approach to his study of a few highly polished Ramapithecine teeth. With a scanning electron microscope he compared the teeth of modern hyrax, warthogs, monkeys, and apes and found that the tough silica crystals in plant cells scratched the tooth enamel as these animals chewed. From the configuration of the scratches on a tooth, Walker could distinguish whether a creature ate leaves or grass. He discovered that fruit, even tough fruit that requires forceful chewing, contains no silica crystals, and animals that fed on these displayed highly polished teeth instead. Thus Walker concluded that the protohominids ate predominantly tough fruits instead of leaves or grasses.

Today these tough fruits grow on trees in Africa that appear in the woodlands at the forest edge. Ten million years ago the woodland trees on the forest fringe of East Africa looked much the same as they do today. So, once again working backward, it appears that *Ramapithecus* emerged from the forest depths to spend his days moving from one patch of trees to another, plucking the fibrous fruits that were his daily menu, and chewing, chewing, chewing. And to move from one group of trees to the next, he must have traveled on the ground.

There are no other clues from the remains of *Ramapithecus*. No head bones have been found to indicate his brain size. No limb bones have appeared to tell his gait or stance. No definitely identified tools or weapons that would illuminate his daily life have been uncovered. So the reconstruction of the life of protohominids—the missing link—must take its clues from other sources.

Many clues come from watching the behavior and studying the physiology of the other primates. For example, the gelada baboon has two additional anatomical features that shed light on the protohominids. These baboons have short fingers, just as we do. Their index fingers are particularly short and they can pick up tiny objects easily. Perhaps it was because the protohominids spent thousands of generations plucking billions of tiny morsels from the trees at the forest edge that our facile hands of today can mend a watch or perform an intricate surgical operation.

It is also curious that the female gelada has her sex skin on her chest instead of on her genitals. This ring of tiny pink nodules, which descend from her neck and encircle her hairless chest patch, swells and changes color when she comes into heat each month. Because she squats all day, any swollen sex skin on her bottom would go unnoticed, but the sex skin on her chest is easy to see and serves to notify the group when she is in heat. Perhaps as female protohominids sat and chewed, they evolved swelling breasts to catch the eyes of nearby males.

Chimpanzees are particularly illuminating as models for the past. Not only do they share over 99 percent of their genetic material with us, but they have an average I.Q. of 80—not far below our average of 100. Their behavior in the wild provides many interesting clues to yesteryear.

For example, chimpanzees regularly pick up sticks, stones, or branches to hurl at intruders. An example of weapon use comes from a film of some savannah-living chimps in Tanzania: A group of five adults is seen meandering along a grassy plain. Shortly they spy an imitation leopard which has been planted in their path. Immediately they huddle, jump up and down, and touch each other while they hoot and roar. Finally an adult male rushes the fake with a big stick and starts to pound. Perhaps when the protohominids started to travel along the ground from one patch of trees to the next, they began to use weapons too—though it would be several million years before they would become experts at making them.

Chimps also make and use tools. During termite season at Gombe the adults go "fishing." Each chimp searches out a termite nest, a large mound of dirt with a main entrance at its peak, and carefully watches the comings and goings of its ferocious little occupants. When the time is right the chimp searches the local vines for the perfect twig (often discarding unsuitable ones), strips his selection of its leaves or thorns, and dextrously inserts it into an entrance of the termite compound. The insects attack the intruding utensil, locking their jaws on the threatening object. Then the chimp withdraws his tool and unceremoniously eats his victims.

Infants watch their mothers go termite-fishing for years before they get the knack. Recently Gaza Teleki, an anthropologist from George Washington University, tried it himself—with little success. As he says, his twig was too long or too short, he stuck it into the wrong holes at the wrong times, and he didn't twiddle it correctly. Only after imitating a chimp named Leakey, an old hand at the art, did he catch a termite—but even then he would have gone hungry had he depended on his skill to catch his lunch. He retired impressed by the talent involved in termite fishing.

Chimps also chew leaves into a spongy mass to soak water from the crotch of a tree. They use rocks to hammer at nuts, and leaves to wipe dirt from their bodies. This ability to make and use tools requires forethought, understanding, practice. Until these skills were repeatedly recorded by Goodall and others, they were considered attributes singular to man. But because chimps use tools regularly, it is now commonly accepted that our remote forebears began to make and use implements from sticks and leaves when they emerged on the forest fringe.

Another thing that chimps do, particularly the males, is hunt for meat. And when Goodall observed two adult male chimpanzees collaborating to execute the sophisticated catch of a red colobus monkey, new clues to our origin appeared. One afternoon, as these chimps lolled about on the forest floor, they noticed the monkey in a tree above them. After exchanging glances, one climbed the tree and sat at the monkey's escape route—looking calmly at his prey. In seconds the other chimp rushed up the tree and grabbed the distracted monkey from behind, tearing it to pieces. Team effort—Goodall was amazed. With just a little bit of planning, protohominids could have done the same.

More often a chimp captures an animal by accident, as when

he blunders on a baby gazelle hidden in the grass. So, to see if our ancestors could have captured animals incidentally as they wandered from one clump of fruit trees to the next, scientists recently walked unarmed through the African savannahs to see what they could capture. Louis Leakey discovered that he could catch rabbits easily with his hands. These creatures watch an approaching person and then suddenly dart to the left or right. Leakey simply leapt repeatedly in one direction just before the creature fled. Fifty percent of the time he caught it. Two other scientists roaming the Serengeti Plains during the course of one week found over half a ton of edible meat, including several live baby gazelles, a blind giraffe, and a buffalo carcass. Unless times have radically changed, it seems clear that the protohominids would have had little difficulty scavenging or hunting—if they wished to supplement their diet of chewy fruit with meat.

Another inferential breakthrough came when Goodall repeatedly observed chimps cooperatively catch a larger animal such as a young bushpig, bushbuck, or juvenile baboon. When the prey was felled, the screams of the captors alerted all in earshot. Immediately nonparticipants in the hunt congregated around the catch and begged, extending their hands palm up, as we do, until the hunters passed a bit of meat their way. Sharing—unknown to primates when they forage for vegetables or fruit—appeared regularly when meat was caught.

Each event was special. Teleki noted that it took all day for a dozen chimps to eat an animal weighing less than twenty pounds. Senior males begged consistently, as did females, while juveniles and infants raced to the ground to recover any bits and pieces dropped. Each animal chewed leaves along with his meat—reminiscent of the American steak and salad dinner—and they savored every bite. When all was over, a lingering few licked the spots of blood remaining on the branches.

The sharing of meat was unconventional too. If a subordinate male made the catch, a senior male was forced to beg like all the rest. Furthermore, Teleki noticed that some female chimps got more meat than others did: *The females who were in heat received much more meat than did those who were not in heat.* I am astonished that no one has yet acclaimed the significance of this: Perhaps if a female protohominid advertised sex when a kill was made, she also received more meat. In the changing world of 10 million years ago, when food was often hard to find, this single ability to provide sex at the right moment could have meant life or death to a hungry female protohominid.

From pondering the extensive meat-sharing found in wild chimps, Richard Leakey (the famed son of Louis and Mary Leakey), Jane Goodall, and many others have cooked up an interesting inferential theory about early men and women. They believe that our heritage began when we started to share our food.

This is an interesting idea. The Kung Bushmen of the Kalahari Desert, among the few remaining hunting/gathering peoples in the world today, share their food to survive. Until modern technology began to influence these people less than a generation ago, they trekked through the semi-deserts of South Africa for at least ten thousand years, moving from one campsite to another as dwindling food or water supply demanded relocation. The men captured porcupines, rabbits, birds, and birds' eggs and carted them back to camp in order to share them with their families. Sometimes a hunting group caught a large animal such as a giraffe. This sparked great commotion among all band members. Hunters hacked the meat from the carcass where it lay while a runner returned to camp to muster carriers. When everyone reached home base the meat was distributed to everyone in an elaborate pattern of social custom. As among chimpanzees, a large catch always stimulated a network of social sharing.

But the meat hunted by Kung men (as with other modern hunters/gatherers) provides only 30 percent of the group's annual diet. (With chimps it is only 1 percent.) No forty-hour week for them either. Planning the hunt, ritual obligations, and politics often keep the males busy talking for days. Certainly no man goes hunting every day. So it is apparent that the long-held theory of primitive man-the-breadwinner is nonsense. From time immemorial, women have provided most of the groceries.

For example, Kung women depart from camp in the morning with their digging sticks, a sling or net bag to carry their infants, and an assortment of skin or bark containers to gather the evening meal. In the afternoon they return loaded down with nuts, fruits, roots, berries, melons, and other edibles to share with their families. Perhaps long before the Kung, the pro-tohominids discovered that sharing meat and vegetables was a good deal for everyone.

And here comes the clincher: If protohominids had begun to

share meat and vegetables, then they had to carry them to a central spot. Females had to carry vegetables and whatever meat they scavenged or caught. Males had to do the same. And how could protohominids have carried food efficiently if not on two legs instead of four?

Since the times of Epicurus in ancient Greece, scientists have wondered what stimulated man to raise himself from four feet to two. Some said he stood to look over the tall savannah grass in search of predators, as chimps and baboons do today. Others said he walked erect to carry tools. The most popular theory has been that he stood and strode to carry weapons to hunt for meat. Only recently have scientists discovered the relationship between carrying, sharing, and walking; now it is conventional to say that the protohominids stood and walked to carry food to a central place and share it with their friends.

The combined phenomena of sharing, carrying, and traveling to a central spot—a home base, if you will—is not found in conjunction in any other primate species. When Jane Goodall constructed a banana-feeding station near her camp at Gombe, gluttonous chimps regularly staggered off on all fours with bananas between their toes, their teeth, under their arms and chins, to places where they could eat alone. Most certainly they did not congregate to share their catch. Some hid. Furthermore, even when these animals caught meat they shared it only among those who appeared at that spot. The food was not carried to a central place for the whole group to eat. So if, as is likely, this practice began among protohominids, the fundamentals of human family life could not have been far behind.

The new emphasis on the primitive sharing of meat and vegetables as the stimulus to erect posture and human family life is in conflict with the age-old image of early man as a brutish, aggressive thug who stood on his two feet and dragged his club from forest to savannah to start slaughtering animals and other men. It is more pleasant to think of our first ancestors as cooperative, friendly beings. But once again new facts from Gombe indicate how hostile our primordial ancestors might have been. Here the wild chimps patrol their territory of about five to eight square miles. Regularly, small groups of males steal along the border of their range, sniffing the ground for the trace of strangers, and climbing trees to peer across neighboring territories. When an unfamiliar chimp (except a childless female) comes too close, they charge, attack, and occasionally badly injure the intruder. In one instance, an older female was attacked so severely by four males that she died five days later of her wounds. Had this happened to one of us, we would have called it murder.

And in 1970 a chimpanzee war began. A splinter group of seven males and three females with their young split off from their comrades in the north of the reserve and began a group of their own in the south. For a while individuals met at the border to solve their differences by loud calling, hurling branches and mock charges at each other. But in 1974 five males from the original Gombe community began to roam deep into the southern territory. Within three years they attacked and murdered all of the adult males (except two who died of natural causes) and one old female—extinguishing the splinter enclave and extending their territory to the south.

The Kung were traditionally touchy about boundaries too. They patrolled an area of over one hundred square miles and the penalty for intruders was death. So, though the new emphasis in academia is on sharing among the protohominids, it is difficult to ignore the probability that at times they defended their range at the forest fringe and even forayed out to pillage and claim new lands. But perhaps, on a more regular basis, aggressiveness and territoriality enabled the protohominids to defend their camps so that they could share their food with their companions in a cooperative, peaceful manner.

These are the clues to the life of our first ancestors: They were expelled from their leafy universe above the ground as the climate changed and the forests shrank between 14 million and 5 million years ago. Slowly they came to live at the forest fringe where the woodland trees were interspersed with stretches of savannah grass. They spent much of their time searching for the tough fruits that they either pulled from the trees or climbed to get. Some probably used sticks, stones, and leaves to pry edibles from the ground, to sop up a drink of water, or for other useful purposes. As they wandered through the treacherous open areas they may have picked up rocks and branches to hurl at prowling enemies. They may have stumbled upon edible lizards, turtles, eggs, or even hunted rabbits, squirrels, or larger animals.

Perhaps they carried what they couldn't eat to a safe communal spot among the trees to share it with their friends. And probably females in heat got more than those not in heat.

It is likely that they defended the area they called home and occasionally even marauded through surrounding ones. Certainly they must have recognized each other, and strangers, and communicated their plans to one another by look, gesture, stance, and sounds.

What the protohominids looked like is difficult to say. Undoubtedly they were short, lightweight, hairy, and tiny-headed by human standards. Clearly their faces were becoming flat, their teeth designed to chew tough food. Most likely they were beginning to stand and walk erect, for this is the most efficient way to carry tools, weapons, or food. The females were as hairy as the males. They lacked breasts, and like other primate females they probably came into heat for about one third of their monthly cycle. And when they were not in heat they refused to accept the sexual advances of the males.

We can speculate no more. All we have are clues. But they do provide a window on the life and times of the missing link—and with it the roots of human sex.

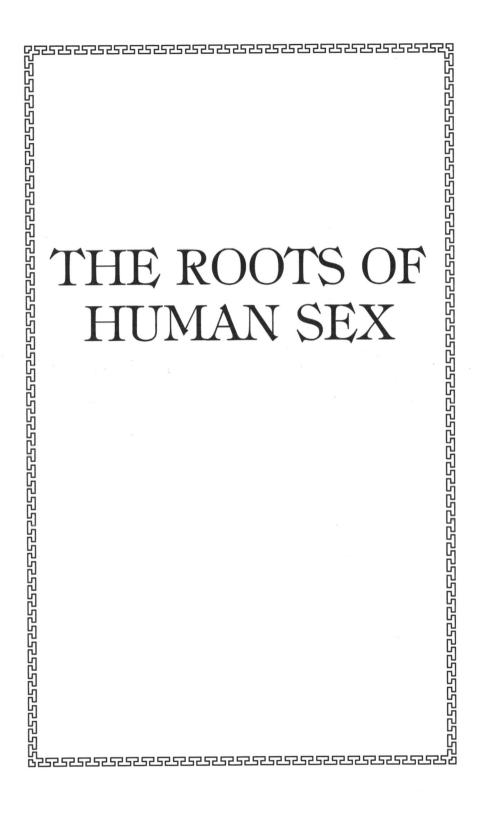

THE ROOTS OF
HUMAN SEX

Let us, since life can little more supply
Than just to look about us, and to die,
Expatiate free o'er all this scene of man;
A mighty maze! but not without a plan.

     —ALEXANDER POPE
     Essay on Man

The day 10 million years ago was dry and clear. The sun had risen above the high rocky escarpments of the eastern rift and bathed the Rift Valley of western Kenya in its shimmering morning light. To the north stood Mt. Tinderet, a living volcanic cone. As Tinderet sloped three thousand feet toward the valley floor, the forests yielded to the woodlands. The mahoganies and evergreens began to thin out and grow in patches between clumps of laurel, wild pear, lichi nut, mango, and other woodland trees.

In these woodlands the trees no longer crowded together, nor kept all below them in perpetual half-light. Although in places their branches intertwined, often they were separated by high shrubs and open grasslands that wove between them. Every day the sun warmed the grassy meadows and poured through the branches of the single-story trees.

Times had changed. Rats, mice, shrews, hares, porcupines, and hedgehogs still foraged beneath the trees, as they had before the woodlands overtook their ancient forest haunts. But gone was their solitary nature. For now the monsoons came only during the winter months, from November to April, and the rest of the year their daily paths were dry. So, in order to survive, they had to band together and to forage a wider area in search of the nuts, fruits, and insects that they had formerly found growing in profusion all year long.

At the base of Mt. Tinderet the deciduous woodland trees began to scatter, just as the forest hardwoods above them had. Here they shaded only 20 percent of the ground, and much of the landscape was open, dry, and vulnerable to the rays of the midday sun. In a few areas ash-strewn land still appeared as bare patches among the herbs and grasses—

reminders of the last time Mt. Tinderet had poured lava and volcanic ash on the land and animals below. But seasonal lightning fires had replaced the soil nutrients almost everywhere, and on this morning in early May, at the beginning of the dry season, the savannahs looked sleek and healthy.

So did the new varieties of antelopes that grazed in herds across the rolling plains. Near them roamed families of elephants and rhinos. Even horses strode the prairie grass. Evidence of geologic change, these tiny forebears of our modern horse had migrated south from Asia by 2 million years before, confirming that the African plate had shifted north and connected with Eurasia. No doubt trailing the horse and other Asian fauna had come their predators, the lions, and the hyenas—the garbage collectors of the ancient world. All now flourished on the spreading grasslands.

As the savannahs sloped toward the valley floors they were interrupted by dry stream beds which cut sandy channels through the knee-high grass. Here new types of pigs snuffled in the bushes, a modern hyrax ate the salmon-colored flowers of the mint shrubs, and small families of giraffes browsed among the baobab trees. Where the gullies met the swamps, hippos lumbered in the shallows. Crocodiles sunned on the sandy spits. Pelicans, cranes, ducks, and geese hunted at the edges of the shallow blue-green lakes. A modern ostrich picked her way through the palms as well. Africa had changed by this spring day—soon to evolve a way of life still seen on the continent today.

Another new creature indicated change as well. She was one of our first ancestors—a protohominid—and she stood in the woodlands of Mt. Tinderet, some thirty yards from the forest fringe. Here three trees clumped together, surrounded by a swath of prairie grass. Their low, gnarled branches were no more than five feet from the ground, and the female remained fixed on all four limbs looking up at the pods that dangled from the limbs of one. Next to her on the ground her infant played with a stick, poking at a tuft of prairie grass.

She looked in all directions, checked the whereabouts of her child, and then rose on her hind legs to pull the acacia pods from the tree above her. She stood three feet high and when she extended her arm above her, she reached them easily. Quickly she detached six of the pods with her fingers and dropped them to the ground. Then, standing firmly on her legs, she extended both arms up, drawing the leaves aside with one while searching the branches with the other. She found two more pods, appeared satisfied, and withdrew to a hunched position on the ground to clean them. Carefully she examined each, stripped them of debris, and handed one to her child. Then they both squatted below the tree and began to chew.

Soon the young mother had finished hers and she was back on her hind legs scanning the group of trees for more. She walked around them with her arms up to move and shake the branches. As she went she swayed from side to side and teetered forward periodically, but her legs were used to the new stance, her muscles were strong, and she walked with little difficulty. Shortly she found a second cache of pods, just three or four, and she walked back to her infant, carrying them in her hands. Together they once again hunched and chewed until the last of the pods was gone.

By now the sun was high. The acacia boughs provided a welcome shelter from the relentless rays that heated her thick brown hair, but she was still hungry. These trees had been well picked over, and she decided that she must move on. So she rose onto her hind legs and peered across the woodlands. About two hundred yards away was another group of acacias and she prepared to depart for them. With a nudge and a cooing sound she got her infant to his feet. He grabbed his stick in one hand, pulled himself onto her back with the other, and on all fours the young female proceeded through the grass toward the distant shady patch.

Periodically she stopped, raised herself onto her hind legs, supported her infant with her hand, and scanned the woodlands. She could see other protohominids in the distance, relaxing below some laurel trees. But with no sign of danger near, she resumed her march. In moments she stepped squarely on a tuber which was firmly rooted in the ground. Though this was a regular route for all the members of her group, they had somehow missed this hidden treasure. Immediately she swung her son off her back and squatted to dig with her hands. Methodically she began to scrape the topsoil with her fingers.

As she worked, her son grew bored with his game of stick

and came to lie beside his mother. Soon he found a new game. He reached for his stick and began to poke at the tuber. She pushed the stick aside, but repeatedly the infant stabbed the root. Then suddenly the young female rose, turned to her child and grabbed the stick. The infant began to whimper but the female protohominid paid no attention—she was intently poking with the stick herself. Digging around the tuber with new determination, in moments she unloosed the meal. Then carefully she pried it from its subterranean home and began to clean it in the grass.

Unconsciously she held the stick in one hand while she rubbed the tuber on the spiky weeds. Then she heard a rustling behind her. Frightened, she rose to see a leopard sneaking toward her child. She screamed, hurled the stick at the stalking beast, grabbed her infant to her back, and fled on all fours through the woodlands.

The young female found the rest of the day much more to her liking. She had raced toward the friends who rested in the shade beneath the laurels and when she reached them she began to settle down. The child was calmed. The two were groomed by the others, and soon the incident faded in her memory.

But not for long. As the afternoon cooled, the group dispersed—each animal going his separate way in search of food. They had always foraged independently when living in the forest and this pattern of splitting up was an ancient habit for everyone. The young female began to remember the leopard, however, and she was leery of moving through the woodlands alone. So she attached herself to two older males who had struck off together, and followed them toward a grove of citrus trees with her infant on her back.

This afternoon the woodlands brought her luck. One of the males stumbled across a hare hiding near a thorny shrub. Immediately he pounced and tore the unfortunate creature to pieces. She sat quietly nearby while he devoured most of it. As he relaxed, she began to beg—extending her hand toward him and murmuring in an inviting manner. At first he ignored her, but as she became insistent, he tossed a bit of meat in her direction. Before the sun went down behind the western rift, she and her infant had dined again.

After the unexpected meal the group headed for the forest fringe—to a place they knew well. Here the branches of the mango trees provided good nesting places. She selected a comfortable spot and began to build her bed. Carefully she wove the branches through one another, padded them with leaves, and settled down to sleep with her infant in her arms. Others had congregated near her and she felt secure in her arboreal nighttime home.

For at least 10 million years the ancestors (the Dryopithecines) of this female and her friends had lived in loosely knit groups. As many as thirty to fifty creatures had shared a common territory, a part of the forest that they called home. Occasionally individuals left to explore new trees—especially young males who had joined up with neighboring groups where they were afforded the status they could not get at home. But most of the females (and some males) remained in the common arboreal turf they were born in, sleeping, eating, chattering, and grooming each other until old age or illness overtook them.

In the forest, meals had been a ceaseless round of fresh delights. When the figs disappeared, the mangos began to ripen, the cashews formed, or the acacia pods hung everywhere. New shoots continually appeared beside the lakes, new leaves sprouted from the trees, and new blossoms packed the shrubs.

So daily they had met where the fruit trees bloomed, or dispersed into smaller groups when food was more spread out. Each individual fed itself—no need to share—and some traveled alone. Often adolescent males roamed in groups of two or three. Groups of mothers traveled with their young, and mixed groups of males and females in heat moved through the trees together. But the woodlands had begun to replace their forest homes by 10 million years ago and the protohominids had begun to come down from the trees and linger at the forest fringe—particularly in the dry season.

Life in the woodlands would place new demands on them. At first the new arrivals attempted to continue living as they had in the forest. Since they were unable to move from tree to tree along their ancient arboreal paths they now roamed on all four limbs along the ground. Although sometimes only a single individual would appear at the forest edge, often they arrived in tiny groups. Sometimes a group would venture farther into the woodlands to a distant stand of trees, where they would feed on fruit for several hours and then return. If they found enough food, they would call the others—as their ancestors had—by shouting or drumming on the trees. This enticed the less courageous out into the woodlands.

Here predators lurked in the grass that wove between the woodland trees. But often food was found and this was too important to forgo. Everything edible was tried. In the forest, individuals had occasionally eaten eggs, turtles, lizards, frogs, or rodents. Some had fished for termites and collected other insects. But these had been incidental treats. Now they were essential to the summer menu.

Everything else the woodlands supplied was eaten too. Those that found seeds ate them. Others watched and soon picked up the practice. Adventuresome ones who encountered tubers dug them up and ate them. Others quickly imitated. When an adolescent ran across a gerbil, rat, or porcupine, he pounced, and soon others caught the knack. Nestling birds, eggs, lizards, anything that appeared before them was tasted—even dead meat. Often someone found a dead antelope, a dying zebra, or a badly injured horse. And if he was hungry enough, he sat down and ate it. If there was enough to go around, others would be called and all would pick over the carcass until it was devoured. In this way the protohominids cautiously emerged from the forest in the dry seasons and began to adapt—through trial and error, through experiments born of need.

No doubt the younger individuals experimented most. An intriguing clue to this was recently discovered among a community of monkeys that Japanese scientists isolated on an island. One monkey, Imo, was only one and a half years old when she noticed the sweet potatoes that the anthropologists had strewn along the beach. Other monkeys had been stepping over these strange, sandy objects for months, but Imo finally picked one up, dunked it in the ocean to clean off the sand, and ate it. After Imo had made several meals of them, Imo's mother tried the sweet potatoes, then mother's friends, and within months the entire band was dunking and dining on the new vegetable. The last to adopt the habit were the adult males. As group leaders, they would have been foolish to try new, possibly dangerous, foods.

Years later the Japanese researchers scattered grains of wheat along the daily path of these monkeys. Imo, who had just turned four, was once again the innovator. She carted handfuls of sand and wheat to the ocean, where she dropped them. Not surprisingly, the sand sank, the wheat floated, and Imo ate the grain. Once again her mother imitated her, then the other females, infants, and adolescents, and last the dominant males. In following Imo's lead, these monkeys gradually got used to the water—an unusual behavior pattern for free-ranging primates. Eventually, two of them swam away to populate a nearby island.

In like fashion, the protohominids undoubtedly discovered new kinds of meat and seeds, tubers, and grasses. Knowledge of these foods passed from animal to animal through imitation. Some experimenters died. Others introduced important innovations.

The most essential of these was probably the digging stick— man's most ancient and universal tool. A digging stick would have been very useful for prying up a root or flinging at a mouse. So when a group found tubers nestled in their trail, an experimenting youngster may have looked around, found a stick, and used it. And once one began to use a stick, others did the same.

Tools had been known in the forest days. For millions of years Dryopithecines had probably used twigs to inspect holes, or stones to hammer nuts, or had chewed leaves to sop water from the crotches of trees. Such tools, however, had not been needed for daily foraging and were seldom used. Now, as the protohominids emerged into the woodlands, these tools became necessary. So the smarter individuals looked around for stones if they found nuts, searched for pointed sticks when they dug for roots, and picked up rocks to scare off vultures from their carrion. Their children used them too, and slowly tool use spread from group to group and from one generation to the next. They didn't actually make or carry tools, however. They didn't always need them and when they did, rocks and sticks were easily found.

The protohominids also began to coordinate their efforts, particularly if a larger meal looked promising. Occasionally they had done this in the forest, but now it became particularly advantageous to cooperate every time the opportunity arose. If three males were foraging at a distance from the group and found an unsuspecting monkey in a tree, they might well have planned a hunt—as chimps and baboons sometimes do today. One creature would have distracted the monkey by sitting below the tree and glaring up at him. Another would sit below the escape route, while the third would go around the tree, then race up and grab the monkey from behind.

Perhaps instead they would stage a relay race to run down a gazelle, or work together to surround a bushbuck and her infant. When they caught their prey, they settled down to eat. The most dominant animal probably devoured the most and portioned off the remains to the others. Or maybe the one who had actually retrieved the prize doled out the pieces to the rest. If others heard the commotion, they would soon turn up. Scrounging would be tolerated, and all would eat in peace.

At first these hunts were rare. It required forethought, communication, and cooperation to organize a hunt, and probably only the smartest were alert enough to execute a successful catch. Besides, hunting was dangerous. Often, when the hunters only maimed the beast it charged them head on. And sometimes the clamor of the hunt attracted the attentions of formidable contenders for the kill, such as large cats, wild dogs, hyenas, and vultures.

In fact, the open woodlands created a real threat to our first ancestors. Here their predators roamed at will, snatching babies, adolescents, and all who were slow, weak, or had roamed too far from a group of trees in search of food. Formerly these predators had lived below them—on the ground. Though the cats, primordial enemies for at least 60 million years, had sometimes chased them into the trees, these primates had grown to know their home. They could leap and swing and hang from branches to evade danger. Occasionally they must have grabbed branches to defend themselves—waving them wildly at predators to beat them back. Normally they simply fled. In the forest, predators had killed very few.

But now the threat was constant. In the woodlands, trees to climb were not only fewer but low-hanging, with big branches that the cats could also climb. So weapons became vitally important. The idea of weapon-use probably occurred first to younger, smarter protohominids who had wandered too far from the safety of the trees. Perhaps one day a roaming adolescent male picked up a nearby stone and hurled it at a threatening group of warthogs. A young female may have stood and shaken a fallen branch at an approaching leopard, or a new mother may have hurled the digging stick she still carried in her hand.

The smart remembered what they had done. The smart watched and imitated others. And with time, the idea of weapons spread from individual to individual. It is unlikely, however, that weapons were made or carried at this time. Like tools, weapons would have been hard to carry, because these protohominids walked on all four limbs. Besides, they didn't need to carry weapons. They simply waved or threw whatever was lying on the ground around them.

As the dry season continued, the nearby woodland trees would be picked clean and more and more often the protohominids were forced to forage long distances from their common ground. Returning the same long and dangerous distance every evening to familiar turf at the forest fringe became impractical—as did the old arboreal pattern of dividing up to scour the land individually. So, much like a baboon troop in the highlands of Kenya today, the protohominids learned to stick together in small groups as they moved through the woodlands. And as the dry season continued, they began to travel farther into the woodlands without returning every night.

Perhaps three mothers with infants and two adult males would go together. A group of adolescent males and females would depart for a week or two, or a mixed group of adolescents, adults, and children would move to a new part of the woodlands for a month or so. At night they slept in trees near one another. When they relaxed at midday they huddled in a group to groom, and they foraged within eyesight of each other. When a cat stalked they would bunch together, jump up and down, wave their arms or branches, display their teeth, hurl rocks, and scream—creating a wild uproar to ward off predators. In this way they lived through the summer months.

Then, as the weather turned and clouds began to roll over the eastern rift, they would sense the change and return to the forest fringe to meet old friends. For months they would travel in larger, more informal groups of thirty to fifty animals again, coming and going as they pleased. As the fruit trees came into flower or the fruits ripened, all would congregate to eat the figs, the cashews, the citrus blossoms, or the acacia pods that had once provided enough food all year round.

By June the weather would change again, however. The trees would produce no new buds or leaves and fruit would be hard to find. No longer could they travel in their large annual rainy-season groups. Once again they would migrate into the wood-lands to forage and wander in small cohesive groups. During this time group members would stick together, pick up sticks and stones to protect themselves, and scavenge or catch small animals to eat along with their daily vegetables.

By 10 million years ago these vaguely human ancestors of ours had begun to roam the woodlands. And during their seasonal forays they had begun to cooperate, to stick together, to use tools and weapons, and, if grudgingly, to share their meat. This first step toward humanity might have been the last—if not for the inclement weather.

East Africa was steadily drying up. Even the woodlands were slowly shrinking. The forests had retreated to the high moun-tainous regions where rain was still plentiful, and the highways of grass that once wove between the woodland trees were expand-ing into plains. Though the protohominids had learned to survive in the woodlands, now during the dry season they were often forced to try their luck on the treacherous savannahs of East Africa. Here the problems that had beleaguered them in the woodlands would be intensified.

Out on the grasslands the large herbivores grazed and browsed in comfort. Ancient gazelles, antelopes, elands, rhinos, ele-phants, and other animals wandered in herds by the thousands. Some ate only new shoots, others new leaves, and some the dried grasses. When one animal group had eaten their specialty they moved on and a new group replaced them, eating a different part of the available plants.

Giraffes devoured the leaves and the bark on the few remaining trees. Monkeys ate the blossoms, pods, nuts, and berries. Bushbucks, koodoos, and impalas ate the flowers from the thorny shrubs. Elephant shrews ate the snails and insects beneath the shrubs, and warthogs fed on underground bulbs and tubers. Along the shallow lakes storks hunted crabs, hornbills caught fish, and crocodiles ate birds' eggs. Out on the plains, mice, rats, hares, and shrews collected seeds and groundnuts, while the wild dogs collected them. The lions and leopards trimmed the old and young from among the browsing herds. And if the cats or rapacious birds left any of their feasts behind, the hyenas, jackals, and vultures picked the remnants clean. The sunbaked savannahs of East Africa were in ecological balance when the protohominids arrived. It would be up to them to find a niche.

Now ingenuity, creativity, and invention were in demand. At night the protohominids congregated in the trees that bordered the lakes and streams. But often these trees were difficult to find. So they slept together in the dried-up stream beds—on the ground. Here the sand was comfortable to sit and sleep on. The bushes that grew along these seasonal waterways provided shade and some concealment. And when the protohominids were thirsty they could scoop out shallow holes in the sandy gullies to get water.

Daily they wandered the exposed hillsides in small groups, searching for herbs, grasses, nuts, and fruit. Small animals became prized foods. Even carrion was a treat. And when all else failed, hunting parties stalked the big grazing beasts.

Because these were larger, stronger, faster, and fiercer than the animals they hunted in the woodlands, cooperation, wits, and bravery were soon at a premium among the protohominids. They invented new calls to coordinate their movements when they trapped a wildebeest. They used new gestures to direct their comrades as they sneaked toward a baby pig. They discovered that sharp stones could stop an antelope and long pointed sticks could wound a young gazelle. Once they felled their prey, they gorged.

But frequently their meal was interrupted. On the savannahs the carnivores had become a constant menace. Often cats stalked the protohominid hunters or groups out looking for seeds and roots. And when hunters made a kill the hyenas and vultures arrived to steal the meal. In the open countryside, with no trees around, it was impossible to sit and eat unnoticed. Eating took time and that could mean death. So small groups of protohominids found it advantageous to haul their food back to the safety of the gully where they had slept the night before. Here they could eat in peace.

They also found that it was safer to carry their clubs and

digging sticks with them as they roamed each morning. On the plains it took too long to find a good stick when they found some roots, and a club wasn't always handy when a lion prowled. So those protohominids that carried, lived. With time they probably invented containers to carry more efficiently. Expert weavers since primordial days, when they wove their arboreal nests of twigs and leaves, they learned to weave bags of grass to carry their nuts, vegetables, small animals, or hunks of meat back to camp.

Carrying was probably the most revolutionary idea our ancestors ever had. As long as they could remember they had stood to pluck the fruit from the woodland trees; risen onto their hind legs to scan the prairie grass; stood to throw rocks or wave branches at predators. But when they began to spend days and nights in the open grasslands it became essential to carry tools, weapons, and food—and to carry they had to walk on two feet. At first this probably was difficult. Perhaps they would stand, then stagger only a few paces the way chimps and gorillas do today, before resuming a quadrupedal stance. But with time and practice their muscles strengthened and they were able to stagger farther and farther before resting.

Certainly the new stance had tremendous advantages. Bipedalism is an efficient way to walk or trot long distances, so they could roam farther afield. Moreover, when they walked, their hands were free to carry more. Their mouths were free to discuss their plans. Now they could gesture signals while on the hunt and carry their tools and weapons easily. Most important, they could cart their booty back to a central place where they could eat safely. With carrying and walking, savannah man had found his niche.

As the morning light cast her shadow on the sand, 9 million years ago, the young female protohominid rolled over to stroke her child. His spot was warm but he was gone, and as she yawned and stretched, she heard him playing in the mudflat that had been a lake just months ago. She stood up, stretched again, and with her big toe gave a sleeping comrade a gentle poke. Then off she strode to a dying stream that still dribbled fresh water into the disappearing lake. First she

tried to cup the water with her hands. Then she lay on her belly and caught its refreshing wetness with her lower lip.

After a long drink she rose, wiped off her muddy front and looked around. The mountains in the distance still held a few snow patches among their upland pines. But below the forests, all was dry and cracking. The rolling meadows looked orange and gold. Often they were interrupted with bare mud hillocks, steep, dusty gullies, and barren patches where only drought-resistant lichens clung to the desiccated earth. She recalled the cashew grove, the pea bushes, the fig and citrus trees that had been her winter woodland haunts. She remembered the afternoon she had departed for the savannah with some friends, carrying her club and pulling her son along. Their journey through the grass had been from stream to lake to gully, looking always for their evening meal.

For days now she had found no meat; almost no one had. Still, the group had been lucky. The shrubbery that crowded toward the mudflats had been full of groundnuts and at night they had sat together, each smashing and chewing what he had collected.

Now that the nuts were nearly gone, she resolved to go out into the savannah to look for something new. Not without breakfast though. She returned to the sandy spit where they had slept last night and retrieved her grass bag of nuts from beneath the shrubbery. Then, after locating a boulder on the beach, she crouched above it and began to smash the black shells with a rock. The nuts cracked easily and she had eaten several when her son joined her. With him—and only him—she shared her food, and together they sat chewing while others stretched and did the same.

She liked this place. It was a good spot to camp. The bushes around the lake absorbed the relentless summer wind. The sand was cool at night and the nuts had been superb. No cats had prowled; no warthogs had stolen food or trampled children. No strangers from distant protohominid groups had tried to usurp their camp. But no animals had come to drink in the brackish muddy water either, and no one had found so much as the carcass of a mole in days. She knew it was time to go.

She looked up to see an older male companion standing on

a mud cliff near the lake. He was staring over the waves of grass and pointing. Two others joined him on the hill and began to point, too. From their gestures it seemed that they had spotted animals and would soon depart to try to catch one.

Our ancestor was ready to join them. So was her son. Though he was not yet a teenager, he was fast, good at collecting vegetables, and uncanny at finding baby rabbits in the grass. When he was younger she had given up hunting, and the two had spent their time collecting vegetables with other mothers and whoever joined them on their daily trek. But now they could both go on the hunt.

They joined the hunters on the cliff and with a farewell wave to those on the beach they descended into the knee-high grass. One young male carried a sharpened stick, the other a club and a grass pouch. She carried the thighbone of a baboon she had found near the lake, and the leader had a rock. Her son carried nothing. They walked single file over an animal trail.

The morning rolled along. The sun beat down, and she began to wonder if she had made a mistake. The brown hair on her neck and back was soaked with sweat. The shimmering heat made it hard to see, and every time she heard a rustle in the grass she jumped in fright. But she could see the prey, a herd of gemsbok that had appeared from nowhere overnight. They looked hot, too, and she hoped that from among them a weary creature would drop to rest in a convenient spot for her and her companions to attack.

Shortly they stopped and squatted in the grass. The group leader was staring at a mother gemsbok and her infant that were grazing nearby. With a circling motion of his hand it was established that they should try to surround her. Our female protohominid was as big and strong as her companions and she gripped her club—hoping that she would have the opportunity to use it.

Both mother and infant gemsbok were looking carefully for lichen and they didn't notice the five protohominids sneaking around them. Then suddenly the mother herbivore heard a noise and with one walleye saw the uninvited guests. In moments she and her infant disappeared into the center of the herd.

All morning the hunting party stalked the gemsbok. All morning they failed to get one. Finally they gave up and headed back toward the sand spit by the lake. Now they needed vegetables and they fanned out into the grass to look carefully on the ground. The female found some melons and her son caught a good-sized rabbit before the day was through. But they didn't sit down and gorge. They had learned that he who lingers in the grasslands provides someone else with dinner, so they trudged back to the sand spit, each lugging his evening meal.

They returned none too soon. An adolescent had caught a porcupine and everyone was begging tiny pieces. Our female had only one bite before it was gone. Then her son displayed the rabbit and all eyes turned to him. He ate most of it, gave some to his mother, and a small piece to everyone else. Only these meat delicacies were shared, and when the rabbit had been devoured the sharing ceased. Each individual turned to what he had gathered and ate alone.

But except for meat, sharing was unimportant. Our female was self-sufficient. She could gather her own vegetables any time she pleased. Often she had carted home small animals too. *So she never needed others to help her feed her son.*

After the meal she groomed her child while one of the adolescent males groomed her. Then she curled up on the cool sand and feel asleep. Once during the night she dreamt of falling from a tree and woke up with a jerk. Then she nudged herself farther into the sand, not to wake till dawn.

Perhaps the protohominids would have continued living like this forever. What more did they need for life on the sunbaked plains? As a group they were able to protect themselves. They scavenged regularly. Often they caught small animals individually. Occasionally they banded together to catch larger game. And when meat was acquired, it was shared. More normally each creature gathered vegetables, congregated, and ate alone quite happily. There was no need for fancier tools, more deadly weapons, or a more elaborate system of communication—just as there isn't for today's savannah baboons or chimps. But a twist of biology was to thrust them along the road toward modern man. Habitual carrying had forced them onto two legs instead of four and the ensuing genetic changes would eventually produce the sexy creatures we are today.

Walking was selecting for changes in protohominid skeletons. Their feet were becoming flat. Their big toes were rotating and had begun to lie parallel with the other toes—providing a platform for upright stance. Their ankles had strengthened. Their knees had rotated inward to lie below the midline of their hips. And their pelvises had realigned and strengthened to bear the weight of their upper frames. Unlike their ancestors, they didn't waddle or sway from side to side as they walked through the savannahs or below the woodland trees. Instead they strode. But the new stance and evolved skeleton created complications for females, complications that were to set them on the road to human life.

With the reshaping of their pelvises, the diameters of their birth canals reduced in size—no longer permitting easy passage of their young. * Gradually, most females would experience difficult births and many died delivering their young. Natural selection stepped in.

In all living groups of organisms, there is variation between individuals. And among the protohominids a few females displayed an unusual genetic trait: They bore their young too soon. Under different circumstances the genetic capacity to deliver premature infants would have been undesirable, but among our first ancestors this quirk became essential to survival. These mothers delivered infants with smaller heads—heads that easily navigated the shrinking birth canal. For these mothers birth was

---

* Because this is a critical point and little-known fact, I wish to cite my sources: Dr. Walter Leutenegger (1974) confirms that the sagittal (front-to-back) diameter of the pelvic inlet shortened as a side effect of adaptation to habitual bipedalism. Though fossil material is not complete enough to measure it, the transverse (side-to-side) diameter of the pelvic inlet also could have shortened due to adaptation to bipedalism (Leutenegger, 1977). I hypothesize that the cranial dimensions of protohominid newborns exceeded or came close to the corresponding diameter of the protohominid female pelvic inlet, as is the case in many species of modern primates. Thus, it is probable that shortening of one or both pelvic diameters caused obstetrical difficulties for most protohominid females.

easier. They lived. Their infants lived. And gradually the descendants of these females proliferated in the protohominid population.

Nature had solved the problem. But now females were left with a new burden—premature infants who would require many extra months or even years of care. In former days, when protohominids had traveled through the woodlands on all fours, each female had easily delivered her infant in the presence and security of the group. She had cleaned the infant by herself, suckled it, secured it to her chest, where it held on naturally, and continued with her day of foraging. At first, new mothers would be less mobile than their comrades. They wouldn't join a hunt. They would travel with other collectors instead. And until their children learned to keep up, they would eat vegetables, carrion, and the little animals they found themselves.

But now their infants were premature and more vulnerable. They had to be fed and protected much longer. Moreover, because the protohominids walked upright, females had to carry their infants or strap them to their backs. It was harder for them to catch their own meat. Often they missed the mouse or had to forgo the run to catch a rabbit. More and more often females and their infants went hungry; more and more often the infants ended up in a leopard's jaws.

Gone were the days when female protohominids could independently cope with their young. Now they would be forced to make a deal with males. With this bargain the sex contract would begin.

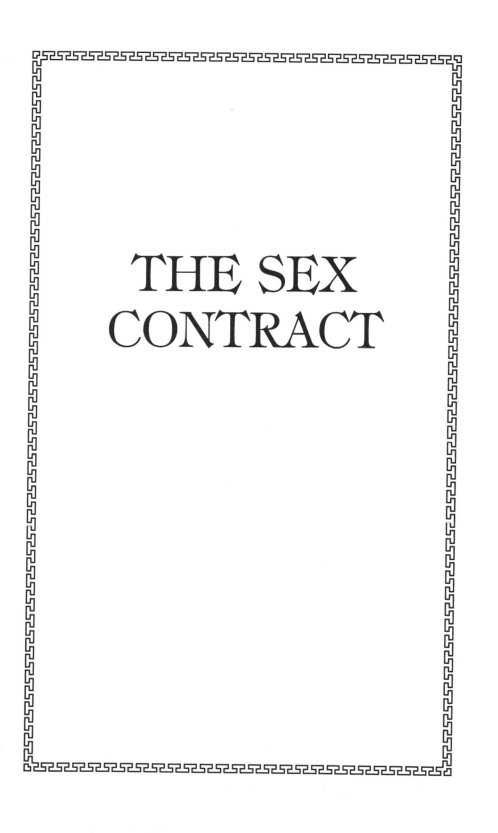

THE SEX
CONTRACT

It is assumed that the woman must wait, motionless, until she is wooed. Nay, she often does wait motionless. That is how the spider waits for the fly. But the spider spins her web. And if the fly, like my hero, shews a strength that promises to extricate him, how swiftly does she abandon her pretence of passiveness, and openly fling coil after coil about him until he is secured forever!

—George Bernard Shaw
From the introduction to *Man and Superman*

"At first, men lived like beasts, without the plow and without iron tools with which to work the fields, plant, or cut down trees. These early men ate only what the sun and rain provided: they lacked clothing and built no permanent houses, but lived, instead, in caves and in brushwood shelters. Lacking the institution of marriage, they followed a career of sexual promiscuity." So wrote Lucretius, a Roman philosopher of the first century A.D.

The idea of primitive promiscuity has been popular ever since. In 1877, Lewis Henry Morgan, an influential American anthropologist, said that the first men and women lived in primeval hordes and that they spent their days engaging in random sexual affairs. Darwin and Freud supported this view, and today anthropologists such as Robin Fox, Lionel Tiger, Richard Leakey, and many others believe that at the inception of the human line men and women were promiscuous.

They are probably right. Chimpanzees are promiscuous. So are gorillas, orangutans, and every other higher primate except the gibbon and its first cousin, the siamang.

So there is every reason to think we were promiscuous in the dim days of our first beginnings. That we have not yet totally shed this habit is obvious. But when protohominid females started to struggle to raise their young they began to look around for help. Everywhere was an untapped working force, a cornucopia, a gold mine—protohominid males. They needed only to woo these males into helping them and their young survive. But to charm them into a parental commitment would require more than wits. It would demand a sexual revolution—the most spectacular the world would ever witness.

In the beginning, all protohominid females experienced a

period of estrus. During that time in the middle of their monthly menstrual cycle they would come into heat and behave sexually. This began a few days after menses. Some would flirt with the males in their social group, touching them, frolicking around them, and presenting their genitals. But only the younger, less experienced males would court a female at the beginning of her estrus.

By the twelfth or fourteenth day, however—during the time when each female ovulated—she reached a peak in her monthly period of heat. Then she became sexually aggressive. If this period occurred during the wet season she would be in the woodlands, probably standing below some fruit trees with a few companions. When she finished eating in the morning she would settle in a shady spot and cavort with the males who now congregated around her. She knew them all. Most were friends. Some were dominant older males. A few had recently joined the group.

If she was a relaxed, experienced female, she may have moved from one to another, patting each, touching and fondling them or rubbing her genitals against them. If not, she simply waited for one to step up, inspect her genitals, groom her briefly, and initiate intercourse. Some she probably received while lying on her back, permitting them to copulate face-to-face. Others she may have accepted while sitting on their laps. But most often she crouched on all four limbs, inviting coitus from behind. When she became tired she relaxed and allowed her most recent partner to groom her.

As midday passed, the estrus female would resume her feeding, remaining where she was if the food was plentiful or moving to another patch of trees if none was left. If she elected to depart, no doubt some of her retinue chose to do the same. Perhaps as many as three or four would come along. Together they would walk to another place to eat. But by afternoon, newcomers would arrive and most likely she would engage in more sex later in the day.

When a female came into heat during the dry season the males stuck close to her on the open plains instead. Undoubtedly she would wake up in a gully where the thick brush was protective and water plentiful beneath the sand. Here she may have begun intercourse early in the morning. As she prepared to depart into the open countryside her lovers did the same. Wherever the group went, she was in the middle—surrounded by males. When she rested, she had intercourse with them. At midday she passed her favors out. And again that evening she would initiate sex back at camp.

For the average female this period of sexual activity lasted about ten days. Then, a few days after ovulation, her sexual desire would disappear and she would travel without a retinue until her estrus returned next month—if it did. A mature, healthy female normally had only a few monthly cycles before she became pregnant. Then her sexual behavior would stop. During pregnancy she would refuse to receive a male and after the infant was born she normally devoted at least the next two years to nursing it. After she had weaned her child, her monthly menstrual cycle would return, her sexual desire would reappear, and for about ten days of every month she would copulate again.

This is the general primate pattern and there is no reason to think that most of our first ancestors were anything short of normal in their sexual affairs. But not all. Variations always exist between members of a species, and when it comes to sex, behavior can differ markedly from one individual to the next. For example, some female baboons have unusually long cycles accompanied by an extended period of heat each month. Some female orangutans receive males during the first few months of pregnancy. And to the astonishment of researchers at the chimp reserve in Tanzania, Flo once resumed sexual behavior—though only for one day—before she weaned her infant, Flint.

And so it was among the female protohominids—some were sexier than others. A few females had unusually long monthly cycles, remaining in heat for as long as two to three weeks. Some had the outstanding ability and inclination to copulate during much of their pregnancy. A few resumed sexual behavior months or even years before they weaned their young.

In former days these females had no particular advantages. They simply engaged in sex more often than did normal females. But by 8 million years ago, the more amorous females acquired enormous benefits—particularly as new mothers. Why? Because this was a crucial time in human evolution—a time when the complications of walking had selected for protohominid females who bore their young too soon. Now all the females had to carry, protect, and feed their young for longer and longer periods of time. But those females who came back into heat soon after delivering their young received the attentions of an entourage of suitors. Everywhere they went they were in the middle of the group. This had tremendous gains.

If a new mother came into heat, her day began with sex. When she left camp, attendant males followed her. Where she roamed, they followed. Where she stopped, they stopped. Though her infant was laid down when she had sex with the males, it always remained in the center of the group—where no predator could grab it. Furthermore, the meals were good. If a male carted an eland back to camp in the evening, everyone begged. But she received extra meat—just as chimps in estrus get more meat than do nonestrus chimps today.

Life without these gratuities was much more difficult. Most new mothers had no period of heat. They struck off together in the morning carrying their clubs, bags, digging sticks, and infants. Often older males and adolescents accompanied them. But normally during the day they depended upon themselves to protect their young. While these sexually inactive females found eggs, nestling birds, turtles, and lizards just as sexy new mothers did, they seldom received a larger piece of meat. They couldn't hunt for it themselves, and when males brought some back to camp, even insistent begging brought them little—much less than their friends in estrus received. Their children got almost none.

Thus the new mother who came into heat soon after parturition received extra meat and protection for the part of every month she provided sex. These profits she shared with her infant. And because of these special benefits, her baby had a better chance to live to adulthood than did the infants of nonestrus mothers. More of the infants of sexier mothers did live, grow up, and breed—passing this genetic anomaly to a greater percentage of the next generation. Selection had begun to favor those unusual females who resumed sexual activity soon after delivering their young.

Like these females, those who offered sex during pregnancy received the benefits of male attention too. When meat was hauled back to a central spot, these females got more meat than did pregnant females who couldn't offer sex. Furthermore, while these females foraged, a group of males followed. So they also got more protection on the savannah. Thus more of these females lived through the vulnerable period of pregnancy. They bore more young. Their young had these same genetic traits. And with time, females who engaged in sex during pregnancy proliferated in the protohominid population.

Last but far from least were those females who were not burdened with child-rearing duties. Either they had just matured or their children were old enough to take care of themselves and they had not yet conceived again. When these females came into estrus they traveled with the males. Among them were a few who had a slightly longer period of heat each month. Because they were in estrus longer, they acquired more meat and more protection than females with shorter cycles. Thus they were better fed, died less often of disease or predation, and produced more young. This way the next generation received a disproportionately high number of individuals who carried the genetic trait for a longer period of heat each month.

There you have it. As generations passed, selection gradually produced more and more female protohominids who copulated for a longer period of their monthly cycle; who made love during pregnancy; who had sex sooner after parturition. Protohominid females were beginning to lose their period of heat. With this, daily life began to change again.

The forest was no longer a memory in the minds of the protohominids who picked their way through the prickly grass one afternoon 8 million years ago. Though the seasons came and went, no one thought of walking to the trees above them on the sloping mountain sides. And though a strange nostalgia for the forest may have lingered among a few, those in the group today were looking down for roots and tubers, or across the grass for animals, not up for fruit or blossoms.

Out on the plains, summertime groups had become permanent bands of males, females, and children who knew each other well. Around our group were others they sometimes met at communal water holes, at lakeside camps, or on the open plains. Often adolescent males or females switched bands when two groups met. Sometimes an older male left one group to join another. And when the band became too large, two or three females, their children, and some males struck off alone. When the weather was good or food plentiful some groups assembled. When it turned dry they split up again. This way individuals came to know the five hundred or so protohominids who traveled in their mutual homeland on the rolling plains. They also came to recognize the strangers who roamed beyond their own turf. Some were friendly, others belligerent. But they tried to avoid the strangers as much as possible.

Our group was moving en masse to a new campsite and everyone was present—four males, five females, and seven children in all. Among them was an aging female protohominid I'll call Hoot. She was an amiable creature, slight of build and with thinning pelt. She had a torn ear, and scars on her knees and back from making love, but ever since teenage she had been a celebrity with the men.

When she first came into heat and began to flirt, tip her behind, and strut around, males from other groups had joined the band to mate with her. In those days when she departed to look for vegetables, a full parade of eager males followed. She frolicked with them all. And when she returned to camp each night, followed by her retinue, she often dominated the evening with her cavorting.

It seemed to the others that Hoot was in heat almost constantly in those days. That was fine. It stimulated the males to hunt and everyone dined better—particularly Hoot. She was unusual when she got pregnant though. Group members had thought life would settle down. But Hoot just kept on making love. Every month of her pregnancy she preened and pranced, tipped her buttocks, and made love to males.

Soon her baby came. Hoot delivered it in camp, cleaned it with leaves and grass, and suckled it. For a few months she seemed quiet, preoccupied with her child. She desired no sex or meat, and seemed content to forage with the other females and collect whatever vegetables she could. She ignored her male friends entirely.

But time went by, the dry season came, and vegetables became harder to find. As the immediate area was foraged out, Hoot had longer and longer distances to march each morning in search of vegetables. Although her baby was getting bigger, it hadn't learned to walk or eat real food, and Hoot found it difficult to carry the baby, her club, her pouch, and collect her dinner too. Often when she saw a rabbit she was too loaded down to leap for it. Even a lizard was hard to catch. And though the others often brought home chunks of meat, she got only small pieces—for now other females were in heat and getting most of the handouts.

As the dry season became monotonous, Hoot yearned for her old life, her carousing, her wandering with the males. She wanted some meat too. Then one morning she woke up feeling strange. She nursed her infant and then reached for a sleeping comrade and pulled him to his feet. He woke up blinking, but in moments his haziness had moved to astonishment. Hoot was rubbing up against him, enticing him to make love to her. He was happy to oblige and the commotion roused the others. Hoot's old lovers were overjoyed. They had not expected Hoot to start making love until her infant was walking and eating vegetables. But here she was, up to her old tricks months before her daughter was even weaned.

This was no extraordinary day for Hoot either. The next day she was receptive too, and soon her male friends began to come around again, follow her on her walks for vegetables, and hand her chunks of meat back at camp each night.

There had been other ladies like Hoot in the prairie. Her mother had attracted a coterie of suitors and there were two well-known females who distracted everyone at the annual rendezvous near the lake. But none would do what Hoot did next.

She was close friends with one suitor whom she particularly liked. He had joined the group once when he saw them all picking crabs at a teeming lake. He was good at catching game, got along with the other females, and had uncanny patience with children—an unusual trait for a male. He became a leader of the group and a faithful friend of Hoot's. Often he had comforted her, groomed her, and given her meat when she was in heat.

But now a strange relationship began between them. She seemed to prefer him to her other lovers—rejecting them when they came around. Instead, every morning she went to him to copulate and groom. Then, when he went out for meat, she stayed behind and foraged for vegetables closer to the camp. When he returned he gave most of his catch to her. On days when he brought home a rabbit, a mongoose, or a porcupine they sat and ate together with her child, surrounded by others begging for a bite. But many times he came home empty-handed. *Then she shared her vegetables with him.* And the remarkable relationship never stopped. She copulated with him all her life and every day they shared their food. In the years that passed they sired several young.

With the stimulus of constantly available sex, protohominids had begun the most fundamental exchange the human race would ever make. Males and females were learning to divide their labors, to exchange meat and vegetables, to share their daily catch. Constant sex had begun to tie them to one another and economic dependence was tightening the knot.

At first these ties were weak. Nonestrus females, adolescents, and new mothers who had not yet come into heat again still traveled on their own. They still hunted and gathered for themselves. Often individuals still ate alone, not sharing with those they made love with. And many exchanges ceased when the sexual tie broke up. But those females who were able to copulate regularly—throughout their monthly menstrual cycle, throughout the entirety of pregnancy, and shortly after parturition—were able to maintain this economic link the best.

Other sexual cement helped too. Some females were capable of intense sexual pleasure during copulation. A few had the physiological equipment for multiple orgasm. Others orgasmed continually during intercourse. Some experienced satiation-in-insatiation, the female physiological response during copulation in which the more orgasms she has the more she can have and the stronger they become. Some females experienced the premenstrual tension syndrome—a period of heightened sexual desire at the end of their monthly cycles. A few females retained a high sex drive way past their youth, experiencing a peak in sexual activity in middle life. Finally, some females had the anatomy to enjoy sex even more after childbirth than before.

These components of an extremely high sex drive are not necessary for procreation today, and they weren't necessary millions of years ago either. But they were essential to survival—because the males liked them. They were sex attractants and those who had them clinched economic ties with males. These females lived. They reproduced. Their children lived with the economic prosperity induced by male attention, and the phenomenally high sex drive of the female protohominid was passed along to the females of today.

Not only regular, intense sex attracted the males—so did intimate sex. And for this, face-to-face copulation was necessary. Unlike all other female primates, the human female today possesses a forward-tilting vaginal canal, one designed for frontal copulation. Most likely the vaginal canal faced toward the rear in most protohominid females, but once again, not everyone was the same. A few possessed vaginas that tilted slightly forward. These females probably encouraged face-to-face intercourse, no doubt because the clitoris rests in front of the body and in this position it is directly massaged by the male's pubic region during intercourse. For them sex was intensely pleasurable in this position. But frontal copulation had another advantage. Each partner could see the other's face, observe nuances of expression, and express his own. Face-to-face copulation nurtured intimacy, communication, and understanding. It strengthened the ties between sexual partners.

Other anatomical features also evolved to entice mates. As Desmond Morris points out in *The Naked Ape,* they all appear on the front of the body—as if to encourage frontal copulation. Fleshy earlobes, protruding noses, everted red lips (which Morris says were designed to mimic the genitals), and swelling breasts evolved as sexual signals to invite copulation from the front.

Not everyone agrees with Desmond Morris. They say that some of these anatomical parts could have had other nonsexual functions as well. Perhaps. But not female breasts. These have no physiological use whatsoever and biologists agree that their original function was sexual invitation. These sensitive, fleshy, delicate areas expand by one third during intercourse. The nipples harden at the slightest touch, and for most women fondling of their breasts stimulates their desire for intercourse. Perhaps the breasts mimic the fleshy, rounded buttocks that attracted males during rear-entry intercourse. Whatever the case, protohominid males liked them in yesteryear. Those with breasts had more young than those without. And gradually breasts became the norm.

But sex attractants evolved not only on the female. Through female choice, the males evolved them too. Of all the primates the human male has by far the largest penis—much larger even than that of the gorilla, a primate three times a man's body bulk. The width of the normal penis provides extreme sexual pleasure to the female. It distends the outer third of the vaginal canal during intercourse, creating pleasurable tension, and because it is there the intense contractions of orgasm are easily felt. Furthermore, during inward thrusts the increased width pulls on the muscles and other tissues of the external female genitalia. This motion stretches the clitoral hood downward, creating gentle friction on the clitoris itself. It seems that the largeness of this male anatomical part has no practical function other than for sex, and undoubtedly it evolved in size long ago because women liked men with large penises.

What other things might females have looked for in their lovers? Smart males who were good hunters and dependable providers were in demand. Those that could get along with other males and had self-confident, alert, amiable, popular personalities were probably sought after. Large, strong males must have been in demand, too, because today men are on the average 20 percent larger than women—a sexual dimorphism apparent in humans around the world.

Though more ink and paper have been expended on this single male-female dimorphism than any other, male size and strength could in part have resulted because females liked males with these attributes. The larger male protohominids probably roamed with more confidence, explored farther afield, and found more animals in their wanderings. This made them better food providers, which attracted women. Perhaps they were better fighters and better protectors too. In any case, if females preferred large, strong males, then their genes would proliferate, producing the larger human male we see everywhere today. Conversely, males may have found smaller females more desirable. Perhaps they considered them less threatening as sexual partners. So, with time, selection weeded out the unwanted, and today women are, by and large, smaller and weaker than men in every part of the world.

Thus a group of physical characteristics evolved in both males and females to make them sexually attractive. There were other traits too. Robert Ardrey has popularized a sexual phenomenon discovered by Eckhard Hess, a psychologist at the University of Chicago. Hess discovered that the pupil of the human eye expands when an individual is interested in what he is looking at. In his book *The Tell-Tale Eye*, he notes that Chinese jade dealers quote their prices in relation to the extent to which customers' pupils are dilated. Turkish rug dealers wear dark glasses to mask their interest. The pupils of men and women dilate when they see a picture of a nude of the opposite sex. Courtesans have long used belladonna to dilate their pupils, and several twentieth-century artists paint their nudes with enormous pupils. Dilated pupils are sexual signals which evolved to encourage copulation.

Another sexual stimulus is flirting, the stereotyped behavior pattern discussed in the first chapter which notifies a potential partner of one's sexual interest. Like breasts or buttocks, it was a come-on that had begun to evolve in the protohominids.

Perhaps the high female voice also evolved as a sexual attractant. Though the human female voice does become lower at puberty, it still remains considerably higher than that of the human male throughout life. Possibly, like small body size, the higher female voice seemed childlike, unthreatening, more sexually attractive. If so, those who retained high pitch at puberty made more desirable mates. Darwin agrees. In *The Descent of Man* he says that the first females used their high voices as musical instruments and ". . . we may infer that they first acquired musical powers in order to attract the other sex."

The high female voice is a good example of neoteny—the marvelous anthropological term for the extension of childlike characteristics into adulthood. Human beings have many of them. For example, both males and females continue to play together long after puberty. (This is totally unlike the other primates, who rarely play as adults.) But the most intriguing example of neoteny in humans is their lack of body hair, a childlike characteristic unknown to adults of the primate world.

In fact we did not lose our hair; it just became puny and almost invisible, giving the illusion of hairlessness. Could this hairlessness have evolved because of sex?

Ever since the protohominids had begun to roam the savannahs they had begun to lose their thick body hair. For a while anthropologists attributed this to savannah living. They said the spurts of chasing small game, the tracking of larger animals, the long days in the hot sun gathering vegetables, selected for a revision in the body heating and cooling system. Insulating hair was replaced by body fat, and sweat glands appeared to produce a cooling liquid film over the exposed limbs and trunk when the protohominids were too hot.

But if this system was so effective, why didn't other savannah beasts lose their body hair? Because the old system was equally good. A thick coat of fur is protective and beautifully designed to reflect heat away from the body. And having the sweat glands in the mouth and on the body makes an efficient cooling system for the lion and other furry savannah creatures. Clearly, nature had to have a very good reason for replacing such an efficient system with another.

Nature did. The loss of visible body hair had a sexual advantage. With the evolution of hairlessness, the soft delicate areas of the neck, underarms, abdomen, and legs became exposed. Just a slight touch with one's fingertip to these sensitive areas could now arouse one's partner to intercourse. Furthermore, these areas could be seen during frontal copulation. When a female blushed, her partner knew she was responding to his touch or speech. When a female's nipples hardened, her partner was informed that she was getting sexually excited. And the sexual flush that occurs during orgasm was obvious to both. The loss of visible body hair enabled partners to signal their desire, to express their excitement, to arouse each other with touch and sight—a tremendous service at a time when sex had become important to survival.

We didn't lose all our visible hair, however, and what we retained appears as well planned as what we lost. At puberty the hair that appeared around the genitals and under the arms marked sexual maturity. It signaled to everyone that this individual was ready for sexual activity. As Darwin has it: ". . . Our male ape-like progenitors acquired their beards as an ornament to charm or excite the opposite sex. . . ." They probably retained their chest hair for the same reason. That the female lost this hair provided her with more sensitive areas around her mouth and breasts—places where stimulation could easily lead to intercourse. And without a thick mat of hair she could display puckered sensual lips and bulging breasts to excite a potential mate.

A final interesting human feature that may have furthered ties between sexual partners is the tremendous variation we see today in the human face. No two people look exactly alike. This could enable a mate rapidly to recognize and attach himself to a specific individual.

With the development of these sexual attributes, intense personal relationships began to become commonplace among the protohominids. Often a male struck up with one female. Maybe one older male was courted by two females. Highly successful males may have provided meat and protection for three or more females. Extremely sexy, efficient females may have had more than one male providing them with meat. But most often, one male and one female bonded together.

Some relationships would be short, lasting only a few months or a year. Others would last several years or even a lifetime. But each unit was a reciprocal relationship. The female expected that meat would be brought back to her after a hunting foray. She was expected to provide the vegetables she collected every day. These were shared first between the sexual partners. Only surplus meat was given to others.

With sharing would come responsibility between teammates— particularly for her young. This happened naturally. A male who was constantly around a female grew to know her young. Perhaps a child began the bonding process. Soon after birth the infant may have started to recognize the male who constantly slept near mother. After the infant learned to walk he rushed to greet the familiar figure when he entered camp. In the morning he invited this male to play tag, tickle, or hurl-the-stick, and at night the infant curled up and slept near him.

When this male returned from a day on the plains the child begged meat from him, and soon he became used to bringing his mate's young the birds, fish, snakes, baby antelopes, chunks of a dead zebra, or anything else he found or caught along his hunting trails. He began to watch over these children if they walked together across the open plains. While on the march he may have helped carry infants, bags of nuts, or other indispensables. And in idle evening hours he may have played with the three-year-old or helped the infant learn to walk. He discouraged dangerous fighting and he rewarded friendly helpful gestures among the young around him. As they got older he showed them how to make digging sticks or to weave bags, and as the boys reached maturity he took them along his hunting paths, showed them his fishing spots and the waterholes where he hid to make a catch. Gradually, a male who entered sexual and economic ties with a female began to feed and protect her young. *The sex contract had been made.*

Thus began a most unusual relationship—one totally unknown among any higher primates except the gibbons and siamangs. These primates live in monogamous family groups high in the jungle trees of Southeast Asia. Here the male and female bond for life, and the children of the couple are the responsibility of mother and father equally. Gibbon fathers spend most of their time defending the family territory, while siamang fathers hunt for the young and feed them too.

No other primate male except the human does this regularly. A dominant silverback gorilla protects the young of the females around him. He even grooms them and plays with them occasionally. But he does not share his food with them, coach them on which foods to eat, or care for them when they are sick or sad. Mother does all this. The males in a baboon troop protect the young around them too. Like gorillas, though, they make no attempt to feed or educate the infants. A chimpanzee female takes sole responsibility for her infants. Though she has strong friendships with males, these friends play no regular role in parental chores. Among orangutans the males simply have sex and disappear.

Under rare circumstances male chimpanzees have been known to take on the mothering responsibilities of an orphaned baby chimp. Among some Japanese macaques, dominant males sometimes lend a helping hand. Interestingly, the females of this species often deliver an infant long before their previous child is ready to face the world alone, and sometimes a leader of the troop steps in, adopts the older child, and mothers it until it can manage by itself.

But males of most primate species don't bond. It's not to their genetic advantage. Why invest their time and energy rearing young they aren't sure are theirs? Why be tied to one female when they can copulate with many and perhaps have several more offspring? Though undoubtedly they are not conscious of these questions, they are genetically smart to avoid child-care duties.

This is a common reproductive strategy in many species. The partner last to leave the scene of reproduction is left holding the baby. Normally this is the female—though not always. In most species of fish the male must wait until the female has deposited her eggs before he can deposit his sperm on top of them. From his point of view this is purely economical. Though her eggs are heavy, his sperm is so light it may float away if he deposits it first. But while he spreads his sperm carefully on top of her eggs, she flees. He is caught in what is called the "cruel bind." He is last at the scene of reproduction and if he wants his lineage to live he is obliged to remain near the eggs, defending them from hungry predators until they have hatched.

Among seahorses the female actually deposits her eggs in the male's brood pouch during copulation. The male carries them until maturity and feeds them via a placental connection to his blood stream. Among some insects and toads the female attaches the fertilized eggs to the male's back, and among many types of birds the male helps sit on the eggs and feeds the young when they have hatched.

Not so among the protohominids, however. At first, males much preferred to leave child-care duties to the ladies. But when females began to lose their period of heat and to provide not only regular sex but vegetables as well, some males began more and more often to bond and to assume the responsibilities of family men.

The effects of this sexual revolution were huge. Parenting was no longer solely a female chore—she shared it with her sexual partner. Certainly this helped the young. They were better fed, better protected, better educated. And if their mother died, they had another adult who would meet their needs.

Continual female sexual receptivity had other bonuses as well. Once the protohominid female began to copulate shortly after delivering her infant, her menstrual cycle returned. She began to ovulate again. Now within a few months of delivering a helpless infant, she could get pregnant *again*—and have another. Formerly she wouldn't get pregnant again until she weaned her infant. This was probably two to five years—as with chimps today. But now she would have to attend to two or even more infants at once. Though this was a dangerous inconvenience to her, it further stimulated bonding because now she needed *more* help from a partner. Furthermore, on a species level it was a dramatically favorable innovation: It *quadrupled* the number of children a female could bear. Close births enabled the population to increase severalfold in one generation, and with males helping to rear the young, these infants survived.

The result—a population explosion. This had tremendous merit. When the protohominids were forced onto the savannahs of Africa and Eurasia they had to adapt to a whole new way of life. For them this period of adaptation was one of rapid and severe selection. Only the alert, the smart, the cooperative, lived on. At a time like that, when selection took a devastating toll, it was to the advantage of the species to produce as many individuals as it could. Each was slightly different, and if many were to be weeded out, many others lived. Thus close births—a difficulty women all over the world cope with today—helped the species to survive changing times by providing a greater number from which natural selection could choose the fit.

So continual sexual receptivity—or the loss of estrous periodicity—promoted the successful rearing of the young and increased overall protohominid fertility. It had other bonuses as well. Because females were now delivering more immature young, these young had a longer childhood—thus more time to learn. This would be essential as social life became more complex. Furthermore, now that a female copulated throughout her cycle, a male had no idea when a female ovulated. There was no peak to a female's sexual behavior; no time of the month when she was obviously ripe. With continual sexual activity, ovulation was masked. Though not conscious of his predicament, now a male was obliged to mate with his female regularly. In this way "silent ovulation" further stimulated bonding. Finally, because loss of estrous periodicity enabled and encouraged bonding, selection bred for both males and females with a propensity to bond.

All were essential if the protohominids were to survive the most precarious era of their evolution—their beginning. What they acquired in the struggle was bonding, the father, the family, and the female sex athlete. The consequences would be enormous.

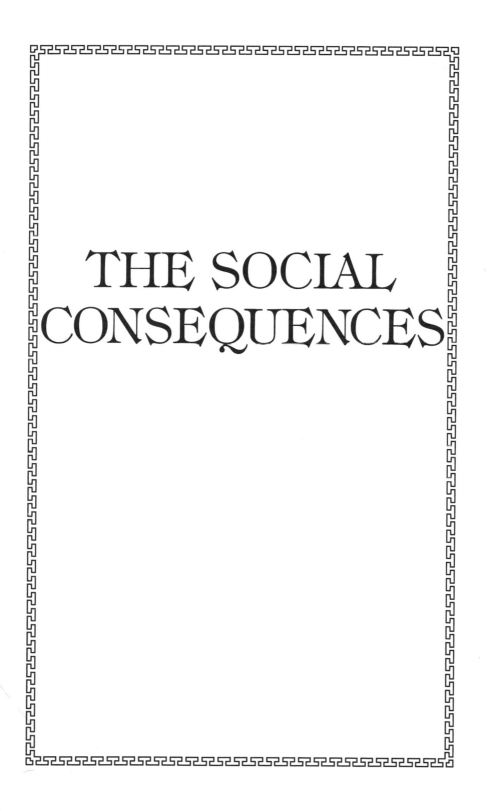

THE SOCIAL
CONSEQUENCES

Among the scenes which are deeply impressed on my mind, none exceed in sublimity the primeval forests undefaced by the hand of man. No one can stand in these solitudes unmoved, and not feel that there is more in man than the mere breath of his body.

—CHARLES DARWIN
Journal during the Voyage of
H. M. S. Beagle

"The blood-bespattered, slaughter-glutted archives of human history from the earliest Egyptian and Sumerian records to the most recent atrocities of the Second World War accord with early universal cannibalism, with animal and human sacrificial practices or their substitutes in formalized religions, and with the world-wide scalping, head-hunting, body-mutilating and necrophilic practices of mankind in proclaiming this common blood-lust differentiator, this predaceous habit, this mark of Cain that separates man dietetically from his anthropoidal relatives and allies him rather with the deadliest of Carnivora."

Man-the-cannibal, man-the-murderer: This was the message of Dr. Raymond Dart, a South African anatomist, when he wrote these words in 1954. Dart had spent years in the ravines, gullies, and caves of South Africa looking for evidence of early man. And in 1924 he examined the skull of an ancient child. As the decades passed, more bones of this type of creature were uncovered in South Africa. Dart analyzed them all. Several skulls looked as if they had received violent blows, and slowly he became convinced that this was the handiwork of contemporaries—other early men. As Dart held one of these battered specimens in his hand he must have imagined an eerie scene.

The annual dry season had been particularly severe this day in early human history and a group of hunters had left camp determined to catch whatever came their way. To their delight it was a female of their kind—one they didn't know. She had pried a large sweet melon from a spot below a clump of brush and under the shade she had thrown back her head, closed her eyes, and was drinking the clear watery liquid from its center. With a glance at his companions the headman jumped from

behind the bush, raised his jagged rock, and brought it down swiftly on her head. She sank. The melon dropped from her hands and spilled its contents onto the thirsty dirt.

The others stabbed at her, too, until the brain was split, the body cut to pieces. Delighted with their catch, the hunters sat and gorged, stripping off chunks of meat, smashing the bones, sucking out the marrow, gorging on the fatty contents of her skull. Then they departed.

Modern people must enjoy this gory view of early man, because Dart's idea caught on fast. Soon Nobel laureate Konrad Lorenz popularized the notion. In a dramatic dual effort to explain modern slaughter and to appeal to human beings to curb their violence toward each other, Lorenz wrote *On Aggression* in 1966. He was convinced that deep in our hunting heritage lay the instinctual drive to kill.

On Aggression sold millions. Here, finally, was an explanation of international war, brutal murder, and our worldwide enthusiasm for competitive sports. Robert Ardrey, a playwright with a bent for anthropology and a belief in our natural bellicosity, soon dubbed man the Killer Ape—the animal who appeared on the savannahs of the ancient world to start killing for a living.

Anthropologists shook their heads. Was it possible—a universal instinct for violence? An examination of the human fossil record didn't prove it either way. Of course the deposit of early human bones found a few miles from Peking contained evidence of cannibalism. Sometime around 500,000 years ago Peking Man had had a bloody conflict. Probably two groups had come to blows over a water source or a cache of food, and on a dreary day in history more than sixteen of the opposition had been killed, roasted, and eaten. The fossil record shows no other evidence of cannibalism.

Within recorded time only the Aztecs are thought to have slaughtered their enemies by the thousands and dined on their sacrificial victims. But Aztec cannibalism is still a hot debate. Traditionally, some peoples in the highlands of New Guinea ate enemies fallen in a raid. This finale was the culmination of months of preparation which served to unify the group. Others in New Guinea ate their friends. This was done with reverence and respect. When a loved one died, his relatives ate tiny morsels of his brain in order to acquire his superior intelligence, his bravery, or his gentle, peaceful spirit.

Does this substantiate a ". . . blood-bespattered . . . mark of Cain," universal to all mankind? Most anthropologists thought not. So, while some fondled the pages of *On Aggression,* others continued their quest for the truth about the nature of early man. They all knew of man's incredible plasticity, his versatility, his ability to change his attitudes and behavior patterns when the chips were down. Few were willing to buy the concept that all human beings, in all cultures everywhere, carried within their persons—on microscopic spots called genes—the tremendous urge to kill, an urge that had to be deflected, ritualized, sublimated, curbed, stifled, subdued. Certainly the tensions of today's crowded cities could lead a boy to kill his brother. Patriotism, propaganda, or financial reward could induce a woman to sit in a factory and create death-dealing bombs. But our heritage alone—with no environmental catalyst—could not.

From this search by skeptics of the Killer Ape theory came the present emphasis on sharing as the driving force in human social evolution. Certainly aggression had its place among protohominids 8 million years ago. Violence toward a hyena stalking behind them at a kill would save the day. Anger vented at a lazy comrade encouraged him to hunt or gather, and scolding a noisy child might help keep the communal quarters safe from predators. Probably strange protohominids were chased off too. But those given to unchecked temper tantrums were almost surely ostracized. Sharing had become the order of the day.

As carrying had revolutionized sex, now sharing between bonded pairs would radically alter social life. First, group composition changed. Where formerly unmatched groups of males, females, and children had banded together, now mated pairs began to move through the grass with each other. It was a logical development. If seven females and three males had been moving as a group, the males would have been constantly badgered for meat. If three females had traveled with seven males, the ladies would have been chronically short of vegetables. Sharing had become most practical between sexually active bonded pairs. So within each group, individuals shared first with their mates. And he or she without a mate left the group to find one.

Mate-hunting probably happened most frequently during the wet season when several groups congregated at a lake or on the plains. Adolescents and other "unwed" individuals then could wander from one enclave to another, making friends and looking for mates. Normally, with all the sexual come-ons both males and females had acquired, most adults would have found them.

Then, when the dry season came, a most unusual thing began to happen. For the first time some bonded pairs began to leave the group and strike off alone—as a tiny family—in search of food. This way they could dine on the fruit of a single bush, enjoy a baby rabbit, fill up on one ostrich egg, and keep going. They could travel farther, move faster, and not feel compelled to return to a larger group when day was done.

Now sharing would really challenge their fist-sized brains. The pair had to decide where to go, where to sleep, when to stay, and when to leave. She might wish to go to particular places where the groundnuts flourished, or where seeds, grasses, herbs, or tubers grew. He might want to travel to certain canyons and to camp in particular gullies or beside certain lakes or streams where animals came to drink.

For this they had to work together. He had to curb his selfishness when the food was low. She had to check her anger when he lost his bearings. But most important, they had to be willing to die for one another—and for her young. As females had gradually lost their period of heat, males had learned to help care for the young around them. But as bonding became a way of life, the males had to learn to protect these young.

If, for example, on a cloudless, scorching day a child wandered off unnoticed, the mated male might have to go look for it. If a bushpig charged the group as they walked through the dirt, he would logically be the one to stand in front of the children to protect them. Likewise, if the male was being stalked while cutting up a piece of meat, the female would be obliged to warn him, or even to divert the predator's attention. To survive the rainless weather they had to learn compassion, allegiance, cooperation, and, most important, the selflessness that would keep their tiny family alive.

When the weather changed they would return to the larger group. Here sharing and cooperation became important too. At these times the males probably went hunting together. Because female gathering had made it possible to gamble on the hunt, the males could begin to experiment and to perfect their hunting skills. Perhaps they began to pool their knowledge of the terrain and plan where they would hunt instead of simply roaming off. Perhaps the older, more experienced males led the way, adolescents were sent ahead to scout, and certain hunters were directed to guard the escape routes of the prey while others made the kill. If one member fell into the river, they probably tried to pull him out. They began to help each other, perhaps even to save each other's lives.

Cooperative hunting required careful division of the spoils. This was no simple matter either. A begging hierarchy would no longer do. Each needed to bring back meat to his female and to her young. So distribution of the catch began to elicit compromise, a sense of who did what and of what was fair apportionment.

When in larger groups, the females probably began to cooperate too. Some days a few women might go to the lake to look for crabs while others went into the plains to search for ostrich eggs or to collect acacia pods. When they returned, they too had to decide who got what and why. Furthermore, when a group of females roamed off, probably someone was designated to stay behind and watch the youngsters in the gully. She was expected to babysit them all—not just her own.

Sharing, cooperation, and the division of labor called forth a myriad of sophisticated emotions, ones we all have and struggle with today. Individuals had to learn to encourage a dejected comrade, to comfort a disappointed mate, to humor an impatient leader. They had to show tact when they disapproved of another's antics, forgiveness when they were infuriated with another's acts. They had to support group decisions they disagreed with, to empathize with a wounded partner, to show kindness to a child that wasn't theirs. They had to learn to trust each other, to show allegiance to the group. But most essential, they had to develop and practice altruism—the devotion to others that would keep them all alive.

Altruism is probably the most complicated emotion we feel. Darwin believed that it was an instinct and that it evolved the same way physical characteristics did. But though he saw altruism among his friends in nineteenth-century England, he could not explain how such an instinct could have possibly evolved. He reasoned that it was not to your advantage to jeopardize your own life and potential procreation in favor of another. If a man felt compelled to risk his life to save a drowning child, this good Samaritan might possibly drown himself. If a woman stood before a group of young to protect them from a charging pig, she could well be gored to death. If a hunter or gatherer tried to rescue a comrade who had fallen off a cliff, he or she might fall off too. Those who were altruistic would die more often, have fewer young, and their altruistic nature would not be passed to future generations. Only the selfish should logically survive in a world of nature "red in tooth and claw."

Almost a century later a brilliant British biologist, William Hamilton, solved Darwin's puzzle. He found an explanation for altruism—and all other human emotions—to have been selected in the past. He called it "inclusive fitness." Hamilton reasoned that each individual shared his genetic makeup with his relatives. From his mother he received half his genes, from his father the other half. If he was an identical twin he shared his exact genetic makeup with his brother. If he had full brothers and sisters he shared half his genes with them, one eighth of his genes he shared with his cousins, and so forth. The mathematics was impeccable. From this, a tale was woven.

In the early days of human life, individuals spent most of their time in the company of their relatives. Each probably grew up surrounded by his mother, brothers and sisters. Cousins, aunts, uncles, and father were often near when food was plentiful. Kin were all around. If an early man with an altruistic disposition were to give his life for the safety of his hunting comrades, his friends would live. If two of them were brothers of the dead man (as well they might have been), each would carry half his genes. These brothers would have children, and the dead man's altruistic nature would be passed on. Likewise, if a woman sacrificed herself to save eight young cousins, she would have saved 100 percent of herself—genetically speaking. Anticipating Hamilton by a few years, the great twentieth-century geneticist J. B. S. Haldane once said he would lay down his life for two brothers or eight cousins—realizing that in this way he would be saving the full count of his own genetic potential.

With Hamilton's interpretation, altruism was not altruism at all. It was genetic self-interest. It was a logical (though unconscious) way for a man (or woman) to save his genes, his heritage, himself. It was a selfish act of self-preservation, a natural way for the fittest to survive.

Suddenly many other social behaviors became explicable in terms of this genetic logic. Sharing, cooperation, generosity, were nature's way for an individual to help his relatives. By helping them he helped himself genetically. But what if early men and women didn't recognize their relatives? Hamilton's successors filled in.

In 1971 a feisty biologist named Robert Trivers provided the answer with his concept of "reciprocal altruism." He said that people help other people because they expect their favors to be returned. Applied to early man, it was a world of "I'll scratch your back, you scratch mine." (More appropriately: "I'll help your genes, you help mine.") Thus, from the biological drive to survive came the social disposition to make friends—friends that would help when times were tough.

But what about cheaters, individuals who received your help but didn't reciprocate? Trivers reasoned that overt cheaters would lose in the long run. No one would help them. They would be ostracized and die probably before they reproduced. But subtle cheaters, those who pretended to cooperate but often didn't, would survive by conserving their energy while reaping the benefits of others.

Because selection would permit deceit, Trivers hypothesized that early man began to evolve feelings to counteract it. Moral indignation, outrage, spite, and the desire for revenge beset the cheated. Sympathy welled up in onlookers. Guilt, embarrassment (or self-deception) engulfed the cheater. Pardon, apology, and contrition resulted from a showdown with a cheater. All were new emotions.

There were others. Because a male was now obliged to defend the children of his mate, he would develop a natural tendency to make sure that they were his children too. Though he might not know it consciously, he did not wish to expend his time, his energy, and perhaps his life for the genes of another male. Thus was born sexual jealousy. A male began to guard his female from other males, to get angry if she wandered off, to become irate if she had sex with others, perhaps even to kill an infant he thought someone else had fathered.

This strategy is not unusual in the animal kingdom. A male lion who enters a pride does so by driving off its former male leader. Then he proceeds to kill all new infants. Genetically this is to his advantage. These children bear the genes of another male, and if he is to work for the survival of the group, he serves his interests best if he works to save his own young. Once the new infants have been dispatched, his females come back into heat. The new leader mates with them and sires his own genetic line. Now he will work for the survival of his personal lineage. This is common among gorillas of the Virunga Mountains of East Africa too. Here Dian Fossey has been following gorilla bands for almost fifteen years, and out of thirty-eight babies born during her observation, infanticide claimed six. All were killed by males who sought dominance over the group when its leader died.

Are sharing, cooperation, restraint, tact, empathy, kindness, trust, allegiance, altruism, even sexual jealousy, fear of cuckoldry, and infanticide inbred human behavior patterns? Hamilton, Trivers, and others would say yes. Even the female fear of desertion could be an inbred trait. A female knows her young belong to her, so the desire to kill her young would not occur. But if her mate deserted her, she might not survive and her children might not either. Thus evolved within females a heightened fear of desertion. If her mate wandered off to have sex with others, this was of small concern—as long as he returned with meat and continued to protect his family.

During the 1970s, more and more human behavior patterns began to be explained in terms of genetic self-interest. Territoriality was claimed to have evolved as a natural way to protect one's young. The feelings of xenophobia and tribalism were instinctual responses that were selected to protect the group. Warfare and genocide were logical means of promoting one's genetic line. Even homosexuality could be genetically preserved if the homosexuals worked to help their relatives. To the proponents of these ideas, biology and behavior had finally merged. Darwin's question about altruism had been answered.

In 1974, Edward O. Wilson, a zoologist at Harvard, wrote a book on this new field. He dubbed the science "sociobiology" and entitled his book *Sociobiology: The New Synthesis.* In it he discusses altruism, territoriality, aggression, selfishness, deceit, hypocrisy, fear of cuckoldry and desertion, and many other behavior patterns in species from fish to birds. This was acceptable, but he advanced an unpopular hypothesis in his final chapter. He discussed the biological foundation of these and other traits in man.

All hell broke loose. Within days of the book's publication, the lines were drawn and every aware social and biological scientist knew his side. For an ugly monster had been awakened—the old nature-nurture controversy.

For almost three centuries scientists, philosophers, and politicians had engaged in a bitter argument over the essence of human behavior. Was it the result of heredity or environment, evolution or culture, nature or nurture? It began in 1690 when John Locke argued that all behavior must be learned. He believed that at birth the human mind was an empty tablet, a *tabula rasa,* on which the environment inscribed personality. Children had to be taught to be kind to others, to share their food, to cooperate with their parents and their peers. They learned spite, malice, and revenge. They were taught to fight for themselves, to guard their property, and to fear strangers. No human behavior pattern was hereditary. Thus began 150 years of "cultural determinism."

By 1842, however, the coin began to flip. In that year, the year in which Darwin finished the first unpublished version of his theory of natural selection, Herbert Spencer began to publish essays on human nature. Spencer was a British political philosopher and social scientist who believed that human social order was the result of evolution. The mechanism by which social order arose was "survival of the fittest," a term he, not Darwin, introduced.

In 1850, Spencer wrote *Social Statics,* a treatise in which he defended private property and free enterprise, and opposed welfare systems, compulsory sanitation, free public schools, mandatory vaccination, and any form of "poor law." Why? Because social order had evolved by survival of the fittest. The rich were rich because they were more fit; certain nations dominated others because these peoples were naturally superior; certain racial types subjugated others because they were smarter.

Evolution, another word he popularized, had produced superior classes, nations, and races.

These concepts suited the times. Europe was in the grip of the industrial revolution and the political world embraced laissez-faire capitalism, colonialism, and expansionism. Europeans were spreading out to Africa, Asia, and America, gobbling up land, subduing the natives and even massacring them. But any guilt they harbored now vanished. Spencer's evolutionary theories vindicated them. Even Darwin would call Spencer "by far the greatest living philosopher in England." Darwin's *Origin of Species*, published in 1859, delivered the *coup de grace*. Not only racial, class, and national differences but every single human emotion was the adaptive end product of evolution, selection, and survival of the fittest.

The twentieth century witnessed a bitter reaction led, in America, by Franz Boas (or "Papa Franz"), a distinguished anthropologist. Like John Locke, he believed that culture—or the environment—determined personality and behavior. And he derided concepts of superior classes, nations, or races. With the rise of Hitler in Europe, the most organized racism since slavery became a terrible reality and as a result Boas's opinion gained adherents around the world. Heredity and evolution be damned. It was into this scientific milieu that Wilson's book on the evolution of human behavior broke in 1974.

The environmentalists were horrified. Sociobiology reminded them of Hitler and the social horrors of Darwin's age. For if human behavior was the result of evolution, then racial differences, class structure, political subjugation, and sexual domination were rooted in our genes.

And what about free will? Under the precepts of sociobiology, none existed. Man was a mere automaton driven by his genes. Even kindness, cooperation, and altruism were stripped from man—chalked up to his genetic selfishness, his struggle to survive. Furthermore, under the odious doctrine of sociobiology, man behaved the same way that ants and bees did, for exactly the same reasons. We were, in short, just another animal.

A group of thirty-five eminent scientists, many from Harvard, formed The Sociobiology Study Group of Science for the People and began to air their views. Wilson was called a "sexist," "racist," "elitist," "chauvinistic pig." Sociobiology was likened to a "just-so" story, ". . . a crude science by simple-minded people." In December 1976, the cover of *Time* magazine summed up the controversy. It displayed a picture of a man and woman frozen in stiff embrace with strings attached to their arms and legs. They were marionettes—chained victims of their instincts, their genes, their biological heritage. The cover line read: "Why You Do What You Do—Sociobiology: A New Theory of Behavior."

At the time, a sociobiology film was circulating in high schools. It compared human behavior with that of baboons. Many anthropologists felt the film was indoctrinating students with the nasty thought that we share inherited dispositions with these stupid creatures. Some anthropologists were using Wilson's book in college classes and emphasizing the possibility that some human behavior patterns had a biological foundation. The environmentalists were determined to squelch this development without delay. So, in December, the same month that *Time* featured sociobiology on its cover, anthropologists met at their annual convention to face each other down.

It was a blustery Thursday night in Washington, D.C., and the business meeting had started. I was late. I entered the convention hall hurriedly and chose a folding chair. High theater had already begun. Opponents of sociobiology had constructed a resolution condemning the new discipline, and a bearded academic stood in the center aisle screaming into the microphone. "Sociobiology," he said, "is an attempt to justify genetically the sexist, racist, and elitist status quo in human society." He waved a piece of paper above his head, glared out at those before him and continued. "Sociobiology will ruin our children. It is a deterministic scam, a political plot, a vicious, pernicious disease."

He appeared briefly bowled over by his own words. When he recovered, he thrust the microphone into the begging hand of a girl behind him. She began to pontificate slowly: "I support a ban on all sociobiology textbooks from the curricula of all state universities. I repeat, ban these books. . . ."

Ban books? Was this an assembly of scientists or of book-burners? Sitting there, I was suddenly reminded of the infamous Scopes Monkey Trial—the result of a ban on the teaching of evolution in 1925. Defense Attorney Clarence Darrow, America's most controversial trial lawyer at the time, had thundered a stunning speech to a bigoted courtroom audience in Dayton, Tennessee. He called the ban "as brazen and bold an attempt to destroy liberty as was ever seen in the Middle Ages."

I wondered: Would the issue of sociobiology call forth a Clarence Darrow? Then I heard footsteps behind me—loud ones that meant business. I saw her forked walking stick first, then Margaret Mead behind it, swinging her way to the microphone. The previous speaker simply vanished as America's most famous anthropologist took the podium. Though Dr. Mead was no proponent of sociobiology, she had come to defend its right to contend in the arena of ideas.

She leaned into the microphone: "Book-burning—we are talking about book-burning," I recall her saying. Then she delivered a splendid defense of freedom of speech, freedom to write, freedom to research, freedom to teach, and the American Way. She closed with this: "We are supporting the people [the book burners] who attack everything we believe in. We are getting ourselves in an insane position."

Shortly we voted. I stood up for freedom. So did 177 others, and the book-banning resolution was defeated by 53 votes. Sociobiology—the hated child of a few great minds—would live. Not well, of course. The argument over sociobiology still rages in the halls, around water fountains, and behind the doors of academics. It is still misunderstood, sometimes misused.

Its postulate that behavior patterns have a biological foundation has never been popular. Not in Charles Darwin's day, not now—even though scientists are beginning to discover chemicals in the brain that naturally elicit emotional responses. But why the virulent arguing? Of course behavior is in part the product of environment. It is ridiculous to dismiss this. Behavior is also, however, in part the product of evolution. So I must use some of the intriguing ideas of Darwin and the sociobiologists and apply them to an explanation of early social life:

All human behavior is not learned. Some of it is the result of tireless Mother Nature, who weeds out the unfit and propagates survivors. Through this constant effort of natural selection, man came to walk erect, to bond, and to live in tiny family groups. And via the very same evolutionary process, it would select for certain types of personalities—personalities with an innate disposition to share, to cooperate, to divide the work, and to behave altruistically.

People with such personalities built binding relationships with those around them. When they needed help, they got it. They lived. They bred. Their children lived and passed these traits to their young. Generation after generation, century upon century, millennium after millennium, cooperation was demanded for survival. Slowly a predisposition to share, cooperate, divide one's labors, and to work together became fixed in our genetic heritage.

From these natural propensities other emotional predispositions would emerge. Love, friendship, trust, allegiance, understanding, sympathy, and compassion evolved to hold individuals together. Restraint and tact were selected to enable individuals to get along. Humor probably evolved to alleviate tensions. Suspicion, disgust, contempt, revulsion, and moral indignation were selected to ensure honesty and reciprocity. Embarrassment, guilt, and shame evolved to beleaguer cheaters. Sexual jealousy, the fear of cuckoldry and desertion evolved to glue mates to one another. Tribalism and fear of strangers were selected to protect group integrity.

Each emotion came to be expressed so that other people understood. Individuals smiled to signal consent, friendship, submission, or appeasement. They laughed to jeer wrongdoers or to support the tomfoolery that sometimes unified the group. They cried emotional tears—unknown to any other animal—to express sadness or disappointment. And when one member laughed or cried, the others did the same. Known as social facilitation (more appropriately, "monkey see, monkey do"), this natural tendency to mimic others is common among our primate relatives. When one monkey eats, another does. This way they all do the same thing at the same time and group cohesion is maintained. Clearly, social facilitation encouraged our ancestors to laugh or cry together—and togetherness was the key to life.

No one knows when these emotions began to ripple through the tiny minds of our forebears. Certainly the arboreal Dryopithecines didn't need them. The pitifully few remains of the protohominids (including *Ramapithecus*) who lived between 14 million and 8 million years ago are only pieces of bones and teeth. They represent the missing link and say nothing about complex feelings. Then comes a blank period in the fossil record between 8 million and 4 million years ago. No fossils from this time period (except one tooth) have yet been discovered.

But by 4 million years ago, early hominids (a name commonly

used for all subsequent varieties of our ancestral stock) had probably begun to feel altruism and the myriad other complex human emotions. Why? Because, as two spectacular recent fossil finds indicate, by then early men and women had begun to bond, to share, and to work together. And along with this, social feelings must have evolved.

The first discovery was made by Mary Leakey in 1976. She had begun to dig at a place called Laetoli—an area in Tanzania named by the local Masai tribesmen for a red lily that carpets the area today. She had been to Laetoli before. The Masai once told her husband, Louis, that the area was rich with fossils, and in 1935 they had come to look around. But their work was going well at Olduvai Gorge, thirty miles to the north, and they decided only to walk the area quickly and depart.

Mary Leakey returned in 1975, however. And within a few weeks she found a trace of early man. His footprints had eroded out of an ancient geologic stratum. They were broad, but just like those of modern man, and upon examination they revealed a few minutes of early hominid social life.

The time was the beginning of the wet season some 3.6 million years ago, and intermittent showers augured heavy rains to come. For a month the volcano Sadiman had periodically belched forth clouds of gray volcanic ash, daily leaving a thin film of dust on the open plains below. Every afternoon the showers moistened the ash, and during the cool evenings the ash hardened—preserving the prints of elephants, gazelles, guinea fowl, baboons, hares, rhinos, giraffes, pigs, and hyenas that had passed by that day.

On this afternoon a large adult hominid, about four feet eight inches tall, was strolling through the damp volcanic ash. Beside him was his companion, a smaller (probably female) hominid, about four feet tall. They strode through the muck together, almost rubbing shoulders. Behind the larger individual, another smaller one followed, carefully stepping in the footsteps of the leader.

They were all heading for a small canyon to the north— perhaps to camp by the side of a stream that seasonally cut the canyon deeper. At one point the female paused briefly in her tracks. Maybe she was scanning the savannah grass for a

saber-toothed tiger who roamed the same terrain. Then they proceeded seventy-seven feet to the canyon's edge. Here the tracks disappeared—as abruptly as they had begun.

Mary Leakey thinks that the two adults who walked side-by-side almost 4 million years ago were holding hands; that all three were playing. Perhaps they were. But more important: These early hominids appear to be a tiny family group composed of a male, female, and an adolescent offspring. Perhaps they had traveled through the savannah for months alone, working together to stay well fed, and now they were heading north toward the rolling foothills, where they would meet old friends and spend the rainy season in a larger group. If these three individuals lived, worked, and played together, then each had responsibilities to the family unit. For this, complex emotions would be required.

In the next few seasons of excavation Mary Leakey found the hominids that could have left the tracks. Fourteen fragments of bones and teeth were recovered—the remains of several individuals, all living from 3.6 million to 3.8 million years ago. Though these bits and pieces say nothing about early human social structure, they look remarkably like the fossils found by Don Johanson, another palaeoanthropologist working in East Africa. Johanson's specimens, by far the most sensational ever found, confirm that by this time men and women were probably holding hands.

In 1973, Johanson had begun to dig along the Hadar River, a tributary of the Awash River of the Afar Triangle of Ethiopia. In 1974 he found Lucy. Named after the Beatles' song, "Lucy in the Sky with Diamonds," Lucy stood three and a half feet tall, weighed about sixty pounds, suffered from arthritis, dined along the edge of a shallow lake, and died in her early twenties—some 3.3 million years ago. About 40 percent of her skeleton was recovered, and it was clear from her modern hip, knee, and ankle bones that she walked totally erect.

The following year Johanson found Lucy's friends. The day had begun well. An assistant who had found four hominid teeth in a block of sandstone at the bottom of a steep gully began to dig them out. A visiting French movie team and a photographer from *National Geographic* magazine were busily recording the excavation. Above them, in a shady spot above the ravine, a member of the movie crew suddenly stopped work to show some things she had just found to one of Johanson's teammates. To everyone's astonishment, they were bits of a hominid ankle and leg.

Minutes later another person near her stumbled across a leg bone. Then two more bones were found. In minutes, cameras stopped clicking as everyone rushed around picking up leg bones, hand bones, skull parts, hip, thigh, and rib bones of ancient hominids. The day became a bonanza, an orgy of fossil collecting unparalleled in the history of the art. The partial remains of thirteen individuals were soon collected and dubbed "The First Family."

Apparently these early people had died together in some swift disaster, leaving their remains in a graveyard over 3 million years old. Although at first it was thought they had expired in a flash flood, the geology of the region proved this was wrong. Maybe they were murdered or starved to death; perhaps they died from inhaling noxious gases or eating some poisonous food. Certainly we will never know. But for the first time in history enough hominid fossils were found *together* for Johanson to make comparisons between individuals.

From studying the fossils Johanson discovered that half of these early people were considerably larger and heavier than the rest. Perhaps these were separate species living side by side. This was Johanson's first interpretation. Later he and his colleagues concluded that the larger bones were those of men, while the smaller belonged to women. The variations were even greater than among modern men and women.

This was a major breakthrough. Known as the primary sexual dimorphism, this male-female difference in size and weight is found in many species of primates—notably those where males and females divide their duties. For example, the male gorilla is twice the size of the female in his group—and it is his responsibility to protect his entourage. Female baboons weigh only half as much as their counterparts and they are totally dependent upon males for protection and leadership.

This sexual dimorphism in Johanson's fossils seems to confirm that male-female division of labor had evolved prior to 3 million years ago. And because his fossils from Hadar are so similar to those Mary Leakey found at Laetoli, it seems probable that early men and women had begun to cooperate by 4 million years ago. With these responsibilities must have come the emotional world that cooperation required.

But who were these people who roamed the savannahs of Laetoli and frequented the lakes and wooded rolling hills of Hadar between 3 million and 4 million years ago? They all had tiny brains—no more than a third the size of ours. They had buck teeth, protruding snouts, and no chins. But their bodies were quite modern. They were a short, robust people. They walked erect and had what look like modern hands and feet. All experts agree these creatures were hominids. But what variety?

Johanson believes his finds are the earliest samples of *Australopithecus*—a group of near-men who inhabited parts of South and East Africa by 2 million years ago. So he recently dubbed them *Australopithecus afarensis*—after the place where they were found. He feels that true man, the first of the genus *Homo*, would soon diverge from these Australopithecines.

This interpretation does not sit well with the Leakey family. For several decades the now-deceased Louis Leakey held that the genus *Homo* evolved side by side with, but separately from, the Australopithecines—although he never found a *Homo* fossil as old as the Australopithecine fossils. Nevertheless he dismissed all of the Australopithecines as an early hominid branch that never led to man.

Today his theory remains alive and well with his son, Richard, and wife, Mary. Thus a squabble has once again arisen. Richard Leakey holds that *Australopithecus afarensis* is just an older member of a defunct line; that ancient *Homo* has not yet been found. While Johanson says that *afarensis*, the earliest species of *Australopithecus*, led to man.

The argument continues: Johanson and his supporters versus the Leakey contingent. But regardless of which "mini-line," which distinctive lineage, eventually became *Homo*, Lucy and The First Family are the first to appear after the missing link. And they lived in groups. At Hadar thirteen individuals had lived together. Together they had traveled through the open woodlands that dominated the Afar triangle 3 million years ago. Together they had come to the flood plain to hunt for turtle eggs and together they had died of some unknown cause. The tracks Mary Leakey found at Laetoli could have been those of a bonded pair

BEFORE ADAM AND EVE: Individuals like this female Dryopithecine—reconstructed from the bones of *Proconsul* that Louis Leakey found—roamed the seasonless jungles of East Africa between 23 million and 18 million years ago. Daily they congregated to eat or lounge, but the females raised their young without the help of males. From these Dryopithecines, or their relatives, both man and the African apes (the chimpanzee and gorilla) would evolve. *Painting by Jay H. Matternes.* © *NATIONAL GEOGRAPHIC SOCIETY.*

THE ROOTS OF HUMAN SEX: Soon after the jungles of Africa and Eurasia began to shrink—by 14 million years ago—our first ancestors, the protohominids, were forced to the forest fringe. Here they learned to band together, to use sticks and stones, and, eventually to share their food, to carry, and to walk. With walking would come anatomical

complications that would dramatically change their sexual and social
life and set them on the road toward modern man. *Painting by
Z. Burian. COURTESY OF THE AMERICAN MUSEUM OF NATU-
RAL HISTORY.*

THE SEX CONTRACT: By 4 million years ago the sex contract had been made. Early hominid females could make love daily and they formed bonding relationships with males who helped them raise their young. Now groups traveled through the plains—moving from gully to

lake margin to water hole looking constantly for food. This band has found a dying hippo in a dried-up stream bed, so they have butchered it and are enjoying a bonanza of meat. *Painting by Jay H. Matternes.* *SURVIVAL ANGLIA LTD.*

OUR GANG: At one burial site unearthed in Czechoslovakia—upon which this painting by Z. Burian is based—our ancestors had laid a comrade in a shallow pit, placed his spear and a mammoth tusk beside him, sprinkled him with red ocher, and put a mammoth scapula above the grave to commemorate his life on earth some 30,000 years ago. By then, modern men and women had settled all of the earth's continents, developed elaborate tool technologies, and begun to celebrate the mysteries of life and death. *COURTESY OF THE AMERICAN MUSEUM OF NATURAL HISTORY.*

who, followed by their adolescent offspring, were roaming across the savannah at the beginning of the rainy season.

So by almost 4 million years ago, males and females had learned to cooperate, to live together, to share their food, and to bond. Undoubtedly a complex array of emotions had evolved to tie individuals to one another. These ties would soon define who's who.

WHO'S WHO

I sought my soul—but my soul I could not see;
I sought my God—but my God eluded me;
I sought my brother—and found all three.

—Anonymous

For at least a hundred years men and women have argued—sometimes viciously—about the nature of the first human family. That it evolved from a primal horde in which promiscuous men and women made love indiscriminately was not doubted for a minute. But how did it happen that ancient human beings evolved a complex system of kin—a system of who in the group is "one of us," whom you are allowed to marry, and to whom you have what obligations? In short, a system of who's who.

In 1877, Lewis Henry Morgan postulated that primitive families began as matriarchies, lines of females each of which took their ancestry from their mother. Envisioning early people as dumb brutes with small brains and little sense, Morgan figured that when a male became bonded to a female, he joined her social group; because no concept of paternity yet existed, the children were automatically considered hers. Thus the first form of kinship was matriliny—in which descent was traced from the female.

To support his theory, Morgan cited the Iroquois Indians of the American Northeast. Because these people traced their ancestry from the female, he likened them to the primeval stage of matriliny—evidence that such a stage had once prevailed.

The latter half of the nineteenth century saw other early evolutionists reveal their formulas for the beginning of kinship. Six major treatises, all by influential social scientists, traced primitive kinship to the female, the mother. These essays attributed no generous social status to ancient females however. Because most of these thinkers envisioned prehistoric men and women as similar to those they saw around them in Victorian England, they pictured their ancestral male forebears as aggressive, dominant, authoritarian, militant overlords of these matrilineal families. And they portrayed the females as submissive, weak, inactive dependents who, by virtue of their sexual attributes and ability to care for children, were supported by their male superiors—in spite of the fact that they were economic drains. Many of us have not yet recovered from these stereotypes.

As these treatises go on to say, when early peoples began to grasp the concept of paternity, the males took over. They confiscated whatever power, property, or insignia the women had acquired as family matriarchs and nominated themselves the patriarchs—from whom all their children would mark their patrilineal descent. Finally, many of these speculators concluded that among the advanced societies of the 1880s—their own, of course—kinship had become bilineal (in which individuals trace their descent from both parents). This, they said, was the pinnacle of civilized social order.

Soon after Morgan published his idea of the primitive matriarchy, however, Friedrich Engels, Karl Marx's close collaborator, wrote a paper called "The Origin of the Family, Private Property and the State," in which he, too, adopted the matriarchal theme. Some anthropologists were uncomfortable with this tainted association. So with the decline of evolutionism at the turn of the century, they changed their views. The concept of an ancient matriarchy was dropped like an infected sponge and anthropologists proclaimed that extant matrilineal societies such as the Iroquois were merely in transition—on their way back to patriliny, the basic form of human kinship. Furthermore, they erroneously announced that in no society had women ever held political power. Now the dual role of the human male as family patriarch and dominator reigned uncontested and the matter dropped out of the literature.

It was revived again, though, in the 1960s—a full century after the first go-around. Again men were doing the writing and again they championed males as patriarchs of the first human families. The most avid supporters of this view were Lionel Tiger and Robin Fox, anthropologists at Rutgers University. These scholars maintained that early male hunting practices initiated the evolution of human kinship. They reasoned that early males had to travel in groups, to discuss, plan, cooperate, compromise, and coordinate their efforts to fell their prey. And when they caught an animal they had to distribute the parts. This fostered a matrix of loyalties, debts, duties, and obligations between males and initiated the beginning of male-male group cohesion or, as they called it, male bonding. Because these males learned to hunt in adolescence, on their mutual turf in the company of each other, it was vital that they remain in the same territory, and together, as adults. This they did. They imported their mates from elsewhere and assumed leadership as patriarchs of the first human families.

Early females, Tiger and Fox go on to say, rarely participated in the hunt because they were burdened down with children. Also, because females were slower, weaker, less coordinated, subject to moodiness due to their sex cycle, and, as sex objects, disruptive to male group function, they were rarely welcomed along on the hunt. Thus they did not bond, never learned advanced social behaviors such as cooperation and compromise, never played roles as group leaders or matriarchs.

These anthropologists had a good idea—early cooperation probably started kinship. But they pinned their theory on the incorrect assumption that hunting played a huge role in ancient days. When Johanson's Lucy and The First Family were leaving their bones and footprints on the plains of east Africa almost 4 million years ago, they left no evidence of big-game hunting. No hunting tools have been found. No giant carcasses have been excavated near their bones or footprints. No herds of elephants (or other animals) appear to have been driven over cliffs. Yet these hominids lived in groups, and their teeth and jaws (like ours) were designed for grinding hard, fibrous vegetables, not for slashing and tearing at meat. So what did they eat? Probably mostly vegetables.

That is not to say that men did not hunt. Undoubtedly they did. That's why females had hooked up with them in the first place; why the sexual revolution had taken place. Yet chances are men scavenged for most of what they brought home. Undoubtedly sometimes they hunted in groups and caught medium-sized animals. Occasionally they may even have carted home a larger animal that they had injured with a rock and then chased until it collapsed. This hardly constitutes "big-game hunting," "man-the-provider," or "man-the-family-chief."

But Fox, Tiger, and others didn't know this. At the time, the faddish theory was "male hunting." Moreover, Lucy and her friends had not yet been unearthed, nor had anthropologists yet emphasized the role of early females in family life. So they backed up their argument for the male patriarch on what appeared indisputable evidence from animal studies. These would further denigrate the familial position of the female in human history.

The first animal study was one done in 1913 which discussed the "pecking order," the dominance hierarchy that defines the social world of domestic chickens. It was noticed then that the biggest, loudest, strongest, smartest, or otherwise most socially adept rooster ran the coop. He ate first, was given the most space, and had first access to the hens. Below him was number two rooster, who submitted to pecking by "alpha" chicken but who overlorded all the others. And down the line it went, a ranked regiment of male chickens, each dominant over some and submissive to others. Of course this pecking order changed from time to time. The throne could be usurped by a younger, more aggressive chicken. Number two might lose to number five and a restructuring would ensue. But flexible as the system was, it involved all male chickens, and on any one day "king" chicken could be identified.

With time the concept of a pecking order was applied to other animals. Baboons became classic examples. When anthropologists first watched a troop of baboons living on the plains of southern Africa in the 1950s, they quickly found the boss. He was the baboon in the center of the troop being groomed by three females at once. Near him, researchers spotted his immediate subordinates, two other grand monkeys. Then, on the periphery, beyond the females and their kids, were the adolescents and those subordinate males who appeared to spend their time at the edge of the baboon social world.

Because this pecking order was so obvious among male baboons (who are twice as big as females), and perhaps because early observers of baboon behavior were all men, it was thought that female baboons were social subordinates, that this male hierarchy provided a primitive family structure—a matrix of protectors, sentries, and explorers around whom all social life revolved.

Anthropologists found the same hierarchy among our closer relatives, the chimps and gorillas. Unlike male monkeys, however, who establish dominance by confrontation, the apes often use only display to show their rank. The amount of attention apes get, and from whom they get it, seems to establish who's who. For example, a prime male chimp at Gombe once affirmed his rank by screaming, flinging sticks, and hurling an old gasoline drum around the woods. The racket got every chimp's attention for over half an hour and convinced them that the noisy male was indeed the boss. Gorillas pound their chests, roar, and stage mock charges at their underlings. Human males seem to have hierarchies too—often showing rank with such abstract mediums as money.

It is axiomatic in the world of science that what you look for you find, and with time it became clear to many scholars that in all primate societies males dominated females—both sexually and socially. On these studies Fox and Tiger pinned their evidence for early patriarchal kinship groups.

This is a specious argument. Dominance and kinship are not necessarily related concepts. In addition, this theory reeks of biological sexism, not to say male pomposity. But in the early 1970s it served well to maintain male-female stereotypes and to support the concept of male-oriented first families.

Since then, more facts have come to light, however, and it now seems clear that kinship evolved from females. Though Morgan couldn't prove his case for early matriarchy a hundred years ago, today primatology can. A new understanding began in 1976 when Shirley Strum entered the 48,000-acre Kekopey cattle ranch near Gilgil, Kenya, to observe baboons. At night these large monkeys sleep in the towering cliffs that mark this part of the East African rift. During the day they roam its savannah uplands. For months Strum tagged along with a troop of sixty-one baboons—nicknamed the Pumphouse Gang—until finally the animals accepted her as an odd but tolerated member.

Within a few days of her appearance at the edge of the troop another newcomer arrived—a big, healthy, young male she came to call Ray. Educated in the anthropological concept of the dominant patriarchal male, Strum expected him to strut to the center of the troop and challenge the most dominant male, or better yet, stride over to the nearest female and demand that she groom his sleek coat.

But Ray didn't do anything of the sort. Like Dr. Strum, he sat at the edge of the group trying to look friendly and unobtrusive.

After several days he made friends with a female called Naomi, then with other females of the troop, and finally—*through them* —he was accepted as a member of the Pumphouse Gang. Then, and only then, did he begin to struggle with the males to establish his rank among them.

During her stay Strum watched more and more males leave the group, and to her surprise several unfamiliar faces appeared at the fringes of the Pumphouse Gang. None were admitted without the consent of the adult females of the troop. With time she noticed that the males of the troop rarely made friends with one another. They fought constantly and they often changed ranks or left the troop. This was hardly the stable core of dominant males so long described in the literature.

The females, on the contrary, were well organized in an elaborate pecking order. Each knew her place, her friends, her duties. So here was the matrix of baboon social life—tiny family groups of mothers and their offspring interacting among themselves to form the stable core of this baboon troop. While the males of all ages came and went, fought, loved, sulked, escorted the females around, acted as guard dogs, they gained entrance into everyday affairs only when the females accepted them.

It now appears that females run the social scene among our closer relatives as well. Like the baboon male, the orang male leaves his mother and his siblings at puberty to roam the surrounding jungles of Sumatra and Java. With luck, guile, and strength he will become lord and master of a large territory where he will spend his days trying to keep other males from trespassing on his turf. And when not busy bellowing or confronting straying males, he will wander through his lands coaxing females to mate with him. Among orangs, only females with young travel in stable family units, sometimes joining other females to travel for a while in cooperative multifamily groups.

Females are also the center of social life among gorillas. A dominant silverback male leads his five or so ladies about the mountain paths of East Africa and defends their young. But like all males, he left his mother's group in adolescence, traveled alone or with other males, and finally acquired his harem only by driving off its former leader. Many of his peers will wander as bachelors forever, dropping in on harems now and then for sex and company. Only the females stick together in strong, stable multifamily units.

Chimpanzees have long been considered the egalitarians of the primate world. They travel in groups, coming and going from central areas where the food is good and the social scene is entertaining. Often a young female wanders with the males and it is not unusual to see her leave her natal group to join a new one. But chimpanzee groups are fluid and temporary. The only enduring social unit is that of the mother and her offspring—the family. So it now appears conclusive that the adult primate female is family matriarch, and her relations with other females provide the matrix of primate social life.

And, anything but a shrinking violet, the primate matriarch determines who's who in the next generation too. This was first noticed among a group of Japanese monkeys at the Oregon Regional Primate Research Center. These monkeys had a well-established social hierarchy. Everyone knew his place. Several old females dominated younger ones. Some females dominated most of the males, and a few alpha males dominated everyone. It looked like nothing new. But curiously, the number one animal, Arrowhead, was an extremely small adult male. Moreover, he was missing not only the huge fangs characteristic of a leader, but also one eye. Yet the others always gave him what he wanted. His very presence made them cower and withdraw. In fact, when he attacked much larger, stronger, younger males, they fled. How did Arrowhead become the boss?

Apparently it had to do with mother. In infancy Arrowhead, like all primates, had followed his mother's every move. In his case, mother was a socially powerful and popular member of the troop, so he learned to be gregarious and self-confident around her influential courtiers and her dominant female friends. Furthermore, he learned to expect deference and respect from her inferiors. Then, in adolescence, when his rough-and-tumble play turned into fighting, his mother rushed to his defense. In seconds she was fighting the mother of his contender, and eventually Arrowhead and his mother chased off the lesser opponents. After a few of these encounters—in all of which Arrowhead was supported by his mother—he came to assume his mother's rank.

Evidently submissiveness is learned from mother too. This was clearly seen among the chimps at Gombe. Flo was a dominant, persuasive, sexy female who, in the prime of life, produced an alert infant girl. Like Flo, her daughter Fifi grew up to be an excellent mother, made lots of friends, attracted a coterie of suitors, and assumed the dominant role her mother had taught her. But a contemporary of Flo's was a timid, shy, ineffectual creature who always followed rather than led. She whimpered submissively and cowered in the face of strong adult males and females. Her daughter grew up to be the same.

It now seems that the primate female plays such an important matriarchal role in her children's lives that she naturally inhibits incest too. Several revealing studies have made this evident. One study involved a group of five hundred rhesus monkeys on the island of Cayo Santiago, just east of Puerto Rico. After being introduced to this idyllic island of hilly jungles, rocky cliffs, and sandy coconut-palm beaches in 1938, the monkeys have flourished—roaming freely through the woods, swimming in the sea and forest pools, growing up under the auspices of their mothers and their mothers' friends.

Anthropologists at Cayo Santiago wondered whether the adolescent rhesus males—who had left their natal group—ever copulated with their mothers when they encountered them. So in 1970 a project on incest began. The investigators found that only 1 percent of all copulations occurred between mothers and sons—and these happened only when the son had just reached puberty. Once a male had totally matured, he never tried to court his mother. In fact, he greeted her as an infant does. Some would try to suckle from their mothers, to crawl into their arms or onto their backs. They made infantile cooing sounds and followed their mothers the way they had as children.

The same was seen among free-ranging chimps and gorillas. At Gombe, Flo produced two strapping sons who became dominant members of the troop. But they never tried to copulate with her. Like rhesus males, they acted like children around her. Twice Goodall saw Flo copulate with every male in the group but her sons. Wild male gorillas of East Africa have never been seen to approach their mothers sexually either, though they will sometimes try to copulate with all the other females in the group.

Because primate mothers hold their families together, it seems they discourage incest between their children too. Though there are no long-term studies to prove it, an incident at Gombe leads one to believe that brother-sister incest is infrequent: It was during her first menses that Fifi, Flo's daughter, was raped by her brother. She fought like mad, and the moment it was over she fled, furious and screaming. Though Fifi eventually copulated with every other male, she never again let her brother touch her.

A revealing study of communal living on an Israeli kibbutz indicates that human children who grow up together do not mate either. Here infants were placed in peer groups, where they remained all day while their parents worked in the fields. Before the age of ten these children often engaged in sexual play, but around this age the boys and girls became inhibited and tense with one another. Then, in their teens, they developed strong brother-sister bonds. Curiously, almost none married. From 2,769 kibbutzim marriages, only 13 occurred between peers. And in all of these marriages, the mates had left their communal peer group before the age of six. Apparently, during a critical period in childhood, individuals normally lose forever all sexual desire for those around them.

It seems astonishing that primatologists have, until recently, missed seeing the tremendous influence that the female primate has on family life and on the social life of her community. Even more astounding is that by and large they still think that males dominate females sexually as well as socially. In fact most of us think this.

What is it in our personalities that makes us think of the primate male as the Casanova, the Don Juan, the seducer, and the female as the submissive, coy, shy, retiring recipient of sex? Granted, it looks that way in most primate sexual encounters. Even a small child witnessing the sex act will conclude that it is Daddy hurting Mommy, not the reverse. But need this have escalated to the prevailing theory that all males everywhere are the sexual predators, females the prey? And why do people say that the most aggressive male is the best Don Juan, that males at the top of the male-male hierarchy actually impregnate more women and have more children?

New evidence suggests that some female primates run not only their families but their love lives too—and they don't always pick Mr. Number One. Among baboons of Amboseli National Park in Kenya, high-ranking females at the height of estrus made love with top-ranking males only half the time. The rest of the time they chose males they liked.

Male dominance doesn't always aid mating ability among the

apes either. Recently African chimps at the height of estrus were seen sneaking to the edge of their range to mate in privacy for a few days. Some of these trysts were initiated by the female, and on all of these occasions she chose a friend—not a high-ranking or aggressive male. Among gorillas, some females pick their lovers too. Though older females copulate only with the harem leader, younger ones often carry on with adolescent males directly under the nose of the dominant silverback. And sometimes they permanently leave the group to join the harem of a different male.

But how, if anthropologists and the rest of us have ignored primate sex, have we missed what goes on around us? Women everywhere track, court, dazzle, and capture men. They do it on beaches, in bars, at parties, in offices, on streets, on telephones, on mountain trails, in jungle gardens, and at desert water holes every day and night—and I'm willing to bet they always have courted men.

Irven DeVore, an anthropologist at Harvard, is so convinced that women pick their lovers that he told *Time* magazine reporters, "Males are a vast breeding experiment run by females." What he meant is that by choosing certain types of men, women in fact perpetuate certain genetic varieties in the next generation—those they like or want. And obviously, says DeVore, women approve of machismo. When a woman asked him when men would give up male chauvinism, he replied: "When women like you stop selecting high-success, strutting men like me."

So some women and other female primates pick their mates. Female primates seem to cooperate with each other to form the matrix of social life. They also run their families, determine their children's ranks, and inhibit incest. If the first human females were anything like their modern-day relatives, they did the same. Thus with all this support from primate studies, it seems fair enough to speculate on the beginnings of the human family and its expansion into a larger group of related kin:

When protohominids first emerged on the savannahs of Africa, children probably grew up with their mothers. Mother was the center of the infant's world. She held the child, fed it, protected it, carried it on her back. As time went by, she showed the child how to gather vegetables, catch small animals, hunt for eggs, fish for termites, and make digging sticks and carrying bags. The child grew up under her tutelage—and that of her female friends.

Males came and left the group. Some stuck around and children grew to know them well. Sometimes they guarded the young when leopards prowled, and occasionally they might let an older child follow them in their foraging. But males never gave children food or comforted them when they were scared or sick. Mother did this. And through her attention to her children, they came to see mother as the leader of their tiny family group.

So the first family, that of early protohominids who had not yet learned to bond, was composed of a mother and her young. And because female primates tend to stay in the group in which they are born—as opposed to males, who more frequently change groups at adolescence—it is not unreasonable to picture a group of protohominid sisters roaming the savannahs of Africa as early as 10 million years ago, bringing up their infants together. For each family to have a name, like Mary-and-her-children, and each larger group a name like Mary-and-her-sisters-and-their-children, seems impossible without language. But everyone knew who was who.

Among the females of a group, hierarchies probably existed— some leaders, some followers. Girl children assumed mother's rank in adolescence. Young males, however, finding their mother, aunts, sisters, and cousins unsuitable as sex partners, probably departed at adolescence to seek status, adventure, and mates somewhere nearby. During their lives the males probably became familiar with several local matricentric groups. Some attached themselves to one, while others came and went between groups. These males probably had dominance hierarchies— attained and retained by display—but their position in any matrifocal group depended on their popularity with its ladies.

By the time Johanson's Lucy appeared, however, almost 4 million years ago, females had lost their period of heat and males had begun to bond with them. Males had been incorporated into the family group. Yet these males, lacking an awareness of paternity, had an ancient tendency to desert their mates. So youngsters still associated their heritage with mother. But by now the seeds of kinship had been planted.

Lucy's first memory was of an afternoon when she was playing in a tree beside the blue-green lake. In her exuberance while chasing an older brother she had leapt onto a fragile

branch and fallen five feet to the ground. She lay there, wailing, until one of her mother's sisters picked her up and held her. She knew the woman well. Every year her mother returned to the lake to meet her and a couple of other sisters. They all treated Lucy as their own and she felt comforted in this aunt's arms.

But since then, Lucy had grown up. So had her sisters and her brother and today she was excited. The rainy season had just begun and last night she, two younger sisters, her mother, and her mother's longtime male companion had returned—as usual—to the shores of the blue-green lake. Here her mother rejoined the sister that had comforted Lucy as a child, along with her other two sisters, and this morning all four women had gone around the lake to look for crabs. The males who accompanied these sisters had also set off early that morning to go hunting. But Lucy felt sure that by nightfall all of them would be settled down together—something she found particularly festive.

In the meantime, Lucy had been left behind to care for her younger sisters. Like her mother, she was often strict with them, not permitting them to be noisy or wander off, but today she barely watched them as she sat and doodled in the sand. Lucy could hear another group of females to the north around the lake. She recognized their voices. In fact, not long ago her older brother had joined their group to mate with a girl not much older than herself. Because he was good at running long distances, he had injured and tracked several large koodoo in his life. Undoubtedly that was one reason his new mate found him so attractive. And Lucy hoped that today her brother would bring in another koodoo; that by nightfall both groups would sit together; that from her brother's group she would find a mate.

Suddenly she heard the snap of twigs, the crunch of leaves, and from behind her she saw her adolescent cousin. He brought good news. Her mother's male friend—a man Lucy adored for his gentle, sharing ways—had found a blind giraffe and felled it with a rock. And from the boy's gesticulations it was obvious that Lucy was to follow him with her bags and help bring chunks of meat back to their stronghold by the lake.

She mustered her sisters for the march. Then she grabbed a

sharp rock she had found a week ago below a crumbling cliff and the grass bag she had woven yesterday, and was off behind her cousin. On the trail that wove above the lake and out into the prairie grass, she met several old friends—other females and their children—and she greeted them with cordial smiles. All were headed toward the catch. Because none had eaten meat in several days, they all seemed giddy at the idea of re-joining friends and celebrating with a feast of meat.

Her mother had been summoned too, and when Lucy arrived the cutting and apportioning had just begun. First Lucy and her mother filled their bags. They got most of the liver, some of the tongue and brain—the fatty parts they all liked best. They also got a huge chunk from the thigh—for since it was her mother's lover who had found and killed the blind giraffe, they deserved the biggest part. The men who hunted with him took large portions, too, and soon mother's sisters had their bags bulging.

The rest went to neighbors—the women whose camp Lucy's brother had joined; to the men and women who normally camped near them in the cashew grove; to the group of females and their lovers who returned yearly to the sandy spit across the lake. These adults knew each other well. Often during the rainy season women from these four groups went gathering together. Often the men joined in a communal search for meat, and often the teenagers from one group had left to mate and join another group. Lucy hoped that tonight they would congregate again.

First they all had chores to do. Lucy and her sisters had to scrape the hide. Her mother and the other females had to clean the intestines and crack the bones to get the marrow out. The adolescent boys were expected to stand guard and warn the older men if hyenas prowled. For people from other camps who were not present, the males had to apportion token bits of meat to repay past debts. The children were summoned to collect vegetables from everyone around the lake so there might be a feast. Everybody knew his chores and spent the afternoon doing them.

By the time these early hominids appeared, almost 4 million years ago, individuals were held together in a web of mutual responsibilities, duties, and debts. Mutual hunting and gathering activities had begun to foster obligations between males, between females, between families, and between groups of families. Now an adolescent male began to see that he had certain chores. He was expected to explore with other boys and report on what he saw, to bring back meat to his mother, to show deference and loyalty to his mother's mate. A young girl had to care for her younger siblings—and the children of other females when they and her mother went out collecting. It was her duty to carry meat for her brothers and the older males, to make baskets and over-the-shoulder baby pouches in her spare time. A mated female was expected to share meat, vegetables, sex, and parental duties with her consort—as he was expected to share with her. Adult females felt obliged to protect one another's children, share their knowledge, help one another around the camp. Adult males were expected to protect the group, provide meat, direct a hunt, and lead the group if they moved through the savannah together. Thus, within each social group individuals were beginning to behave in prescribed ways—according to categorical relationships such as father, mother, son, daughter, aunt, uncle, wife, husband.

Here is the beginning of kinship: a social arrangement—implicitly recognized by all—of who stands in what kin relationship to whom, who owes what to whom, and how individuals of particular kinship categories are expected to pay their social debts. Because everyone had begun to acquire duties, debts, and obligations, and to define the nature of these exchanges, the natural categories and concept of kinship had started to evolve in the tiny brains of Lucy and her friends.

With time, a whole set of rules regarding kinship would develop. One of the first was probably the incest taboo, the prohibition of marrying within the family. And for a good economic reason: Picture yourself as the adult female of a tiny family group 4 million years ago. You and your mate have a daughter. Together you raise her. Then, at adolescence, your "husband" starts mating with her. They produce three hungry, rambunctious infants in the next three years. Not only will this cause friction in the group, but you now have three grandchildren and no extra help. Your family has increased by three members—all infants—and no new adults have joined the group to help you and your family support your multiplying numbers.

Economically, you're in a bind. Thus it is to everyone's advantage that individuals who reach puberty either import mates from somewhere else or leave the family to find them. Those who stick around and produce new infants with a parent put an economic burden on everyone involved. This early men and women could not afford.

What about siblings, though? They could mate with each other without economic consequences. Perhaps sometimes they did. But with the natural tendency to find one's siblings sexually unattractive, it seems likely that an incest taboo was an easy one to enforce.

I cannot think of any one social rule that has received so much attention from people past and present as the incest taboo. This may be because it is universal to all human kinship systems, and in many societies it applies not only to a male's mother and sister but to all females of the clan. Freud popularized the question with his theory of the Oedipus complex in 1913. In his version, early man roamed in a primal horde ruled by a tyrannical older male who kept all the women for himself. With time the frustrated younger men around him killed and ate their father, then mated with his females. Eventually, overcome with remorse, they hailed their father as family patriarch and instituted the incest taboo to prevent further atrocities.

A few still champion the idea. Others say instead that the taboo originated to discourage the disastrous effects of inbreeding. The serious effects of inbreeding occur much more slowly than is commonly thought, however, only after hundreds of generations. And far from fearing it, many human beings today hope to marry their first cousins—a practical marriage in many societies. So all things considered, the incest taboo seems to have stemmed from nothing more than practical economics and the childhood familiarity that makes siblings find one another unattractive as mates.

Another kinship rule that Lucy and her friends would probably institute was exogamy—or marrying out of the group of mother and her sisters. Like the incest taboo, exogamy had an advantage too—in this case, political alliance. For example, if you lived 4 million years ago and your daughter brought in a mate from a nearby group, then the members of that group would be partial to you and yours. If your daughter left your group for another, then you would have a bond with them too. Either way the exchange was made, "marrying out" strengthened alliances between local groups.

This could well have become essential to survival—even this early in human history. For without a system of alliances life would surely be rife with disputes over access to certain water holes, fruiting groves, and safe spots to spend the night. As Edward Tylor put it in 1889: "Among tribes of low culture there is but one means known of keeping up permanent alliances, and that means is inter-marriage. . . . Again and again in the world's history savage tribes must have had plainly in their minds the simple practical alternative between marrying-out and being killed out."

Like the incest taboo, exogamy is a universal kinship rule. Anthropologists consider it so important that they believe it to be the foundation of all the complicated kinship systems we see around the world today. For with whom you exchange mates, you exchange friendship.

Though Lucy and her friends could hardly be expected to have begun to marry according to systematic rules, they would soon begin. For with the beginning of bonding, men and women had acquired property—each other. Women had acquired men. Men had acquired women, sons, and daughters. So, along with incest and exogamy, they would need other rules to handle their new possessions.

One early rule probably was fidelity—for more good economic reasons. Fidelity cemented the bonded pair together and thus ensured the survival of their offspring. Furthermore, infidelity was impractical—particularly from the male's point of view. He stood to be cuckolded, to expend his time and energy raising another man's child. Thus, males were probably the first to impose sexual restrictions on their mates. For a female, infidelity would not be too disastrous as long as her husband stuck around to do familial chores. But if he wandered too long, she was deserted. This meant no child support. So females also sought to discourage infidelity. For these reasons, fidelity is probably an ancient rule—though a rule that both men and women often broke.

But I have gone too far. Surely Lucy and her friends had begun to see group members in terms of kin by 4 million years ago. They recognized their mother, her consort, and their siblings—

the members of their natal family. They recognized the larger group of their mother, her sisters, their males, and the other children of the group—what would come to be called the clan. Finally, because any one area had several mother-centered groups, they had probably begun to recognize themselves as part of an even larger social unit—what would someday be called the tribe.

It can be said with some certainty that these social groups were matrilineal—that individuals vaguely traced their descent from mother. That these early family groups were matrilocal (or resided in the territory of the female) is also probable. But it is likely that during the dry season, when a tiny family group struck off alone, a mated pair went to wherever the male knew the terrain (the patrilocal area). Why? Because this was the season when vegetables were difficult to find, and if they went to the water holes, the gullies, the cliffs, and the game trails that the male knew best, they had a better chance to get some meat.

When the weather permitted rendezvous with the larger group, however, it seems likely that the family went to where the female met her sisters—the matrilocal area. Here the female could collect vegetables in a terrain she knew well. Furthermore, since her mate had probably left his natal group in adolescence to join hers, it was here that he called home. And here that he had acquired rank and status among the males.

Undoubtedly the female's group resided *near* where the male had grown up, however, and so some couples may have lived in the male's natal group instead. This might have happened most often when a male had achieved high status in his own group in early adolescence. Under such circumstances he probably would endeavor to entice a female to follow him back home.

Thus a young East African hominid girl of 4 million years ago saw herself as her mother's daughter, as a member of the group that assembled every fall by the blue-green lake, and probably as a member of one of several friendly groups that wandered beneath the volcanic Mount Sadiman. Within her group she worked and played; from among the other nearby groups she would find her mate.

She probably behaved in prescribed ways toward her father, uncles, brothers, cousins, and strangers. And in each relationship there were expectations, chores, duties, obligations, and understandings. But unquestionably she did not yet call her father by his kin name, nor her aunts, uncles, sisters, and cousins by these categorical kinship terms. She had not yet begun consciously to reckon her descent either from her father or her mother. And she had heard of no complicated rules explaining whom she should marry.

But now that the seeds of kinship had been planted, the complicated rules and terms would soon evolve. All these people needed were words.

THE
GIFT OF GAB

Language exists only when it is listened to as well as spoken. The hearer is an indispensable partner.

—JOHN DEWEY

"We walked down the path to the well-house, attracted by the fragrance of the honeysuckle with which it was covered. Someone was drawing water and my teacher placed my hand under the spout. As the cool stream gushed over one hand, she spelled into the other the word 'water,' first slowly then rapidly. I stood still, my whole attention fixed upon the motion of her fingers. Suddenly I felt a misty consciousness as of something forgotten—a thrill of returning thought; and somehow the mystery of language was revealed to me. I knew then that 'w-a-t-e-r' meant the wonderful cool something that was flowing over my hand. That living word awakened my soul, gave it light, hope, joy, set it free!"

So wrote Helen Keller of the summer morning in 1887 when, at the age of seven, she entered the human race. Robbed of sight and hearing by a fever at age nineteen months, she had lived for years like an unruly animal, roaming through her family's home in Tuscumbia, Alabama, destroying what she wished, staging tantrums for attention, sulking and rocking in her crib—detached from humanity by her inability to communicate. Teachers had come to the Keller home to try to work with Helen but each had been scared off by her violent nature. When Ann Sullivan appeared, however, all this changed.

Ann Sullivan was a disciplinarian. Soon after she arrived, Helen staged a throwing incident in the dining room designed to scare off the newcomer. When she hurled milk, sugar, silverware, and herself around the room, however, Ann seized her and held her down. But the new teacher had more than guts. She had grown up in a poorhouse in Massachusetts and as a teenager had begun to support herself and her brother by working with the blind and deaf. She was proficient in American Sign Language, or

Ameslan, the gestural hand language of the deaf. As soon as she arrived she began to train the unruly child.

Every time Helen touched an object Ann would grab her other hand and spell out its English word. For weeks this went on without consequence. The child made no connection. Then came the famous day at the water pump when finally Helen saw the relationship between the new hand signals and the objects she had always touched. As she later said: "I left the well-house eager to learn. Everything had a name, and each name gave birth to a new thought. As we returned to the house every object which I touched seemed to quiver with life. That was because I saw everything with a strange, new sight that had come to me." Helen had changed. She had learned the rudiments of human language and become a human being.

Language is a hallmark of the human species. With sounds strung together to make words, with words strung together to make sentences, men, women, and children express their needs, voice their demands, articulate their joys, worries, ideas, experiences, and feelings. Through language a child is told what is good and bad, right and wrong, dangerous and safe. Through language adults coordinate their efforts, plan their time, discuss the future, recapture the past. Through words the laws, beliefs, traditions, myths, jokes, poems, every part of culture is passed from one generation to the next. Human language, our particular system of clicks, squeaks, hisses, murmurs, howls, grunts, and other mouthy little noises, sets us apart from every other living organism. Even Darwin, who forever upheld the concept that man was simply another animal, said: "The lower animals differ from man solely in his almost infinitely larger power of associating together the most diversified sounds and ideas."

Many modern linguists challenge Darwin. They say that language is more than this, that it is a phenomenon unique to man. This argument stems from their definition of what language really is. As concisely as possible this is what they mean:

Language is all the tiny meaningless sounds we make, like *pa, ba, ss, sh, t, th, ō,* and many others combined to make words that mean things. These sounds—called phonemes—are nonsense sounds. Alone they have no meaning whatsoever. But they can be combined to make an infinite number of words to describe an infinite number of things, feelings, relationships, and phenomena. They can be recombined too. For example, the word *f-i-sh* is made up of three meaningless sounds, *f, i,* and *sh.* If you drop the *f* sound and replace it with a *d,* you get the word *d-i-sh*— an entirely new word, an entirely different meaning. *Sh* can be recombined with *i* and *p* and you get *ship.* Thus, language is an "open" system—using only a few sounds, you can make millions of words.

Some of the approximately four thousand languages known today have as few as twelve sounds, used over and over in different combinations to mean different things. English employs thirty-three separate sounds and some languages employ as many as sixty. This is the limit. No language uses more. Probably because our organs of speech—the mouth, tongue, throat, voice box (or larynx), and vocal cords—can only produce this many.

In early childhood every human being is capable of making all of these sounds. But as a child learns his or her native tongue, foreign sounds become increasingly difficult to make. For example, many English-speaking adults learning French are unable to pronounce the French *r,* and early in childhood we lose the ability to make the "click" sound so characteristic of some African languages.

But recombination doesn't stop with phonemes. Words— called morphemes—can be recombined too. "Sally loves Walter" means something different from "Walter loves Sally." Substitute the meaningless sound *d* and you've got another new meaning: "Sally loved Walter." Now time is expressed too. This way, through recombining phonemes and morphemes according to rules of grammar, the hisses, clicks, grunts, and coos of human beings constitute a language.

Human language is not only "open," or subject to recombination of sounds, but arbitrary as well. For example, at some time someone bestowed the meaning of a large, stupid, grass-eating, good-tasting animal that goes "moo" on a system of noises that when spoken sounds like *c-o-w.* Not so in other languages. The sounds *c, o,* and *w* might mean "witch," or "laugh," or nothing at all. So at some point we began to make sound combinations mean things. We are still making up new words to create new ideas, as well as creating new ideas from new combinations of traditional words.

Thus human language has two fundamental qualities: Its

meaningless sounds are "open" to recombination and the meaning of these sound combinations is arbitrary. And here lies the distinction, many linguists say, between the language of man and the communication systems of all other animals.

Pigs, dogs, cats, birds, fish, every living creature that utters sound is communicating. Gibbons have about twelve calls they make to say "danger," "food here," "let's make love," and so on. Vervet monkeys of Africa have separate calls for differents kinds of predators: the "snake" call, the "eagle" call, the "leopard" call, and the "unfamiliar human" call. Chimpanzees use over sixty calls to express their feelings, desires, or intentions. But all of these animals are stuck linguistically. Each call carries a specific meaning, and the parts of the sound cannot be recombined to mean something different.

Thus the animal "call system" does not faintly resemble human language—a sound code based on short meaningless sounds that can be infinitely combined and recombined into meaningful units. Furthermore, animals do not originate and bestow meaning on new combinations of sounds. You can train your dog to "get-the-ball" but he will never create a new sound that arbitrarily means to you "throw-the-ball."

For these reasons many linguists maintain that language is unique to man, that Helen Keller lived in an animal world until the age of seven. Like an animal she responded to her mother's touch. Like an animal she knew where the icebox was, what tasted good, when she was bad. But she had no human language. Only when she realized that w-a-t-e-r meant the cool liquid from the tap did she realize that everything had a name, that each name was made up of a series of elements, that every tiny element could be reused, reshuffled to mean something different. With time and training she would make her own combinations of sounds and words to express her human self.

Because language is so important to human life, man has long been curious about its origin. How did it evolve? From what did it come, when, and why? In the mid-nineteenth century there were so many rank speculations and unscientific treatises on the origin and evolution of human language that by 1866 the Société de Linguistique de Paris, beset with these papers, decided to ban any further communication on the topic. People continued to speculate but it was almost a century later that serious investigation began—with a look at language potential in our nearest relatives, the apes.

In 1959 Catherine and Keith Hayes adopted a baby female chimpanzee they called Vicki. Vicki grew up in a trailer behind their home in Reno, Nevada. She was treated like a human child. She wore diapers, played with dolls and trucks, and learned the dos and don'ts of the Hayes household. For six years they tried to teach her to speak but she learned to make only four almost incomprehensible human words. Even with these she had a heavy chimpanzee accent and she would speak the words only after a slap on the neck or a punch in the stomach. The Hayeses concluded that speech was impossible for chimpanzees—probably because chimps were physiologically incapable of producing the necessary sounds.

In 1966 Allan and Beatrice Gardner, psychologists at the University of Nevada, watched a film of Vicki and noticed that she made hand gestures when she spoke. So it occurred to them that perhaps a gestural language would prove more successful. In June of the same year they acquired a year-old chimp. They named her Washoe, after the county in which they lived, and began to teach their youngster Ameslan—the American Sign Language of the Deaf. Just as Ann Sullivan did with Helen Keller, they signed out cup, brush, bathroom, dirty, tickle, gimmee, and many other words.

At about the age of two Washoe made her first two-word signs, "gimmee-sweet" and "come-open." Because it is at this age that human children do the same, the Gardners were encouraged. During the next four years the chimp acquired an active vocabulary of 132 signs and learned to make 294 two-sign sentences— no minor feat. She also reportedly invented two new words, signing "water-bird" one day when she saw a swan, and "drink-fruit" when she ate a watermelon. She also coined a new gesture for her bib—the same one Ameslan uses. And remarkably, one day when she saw her reflection in the mirror she signed "me-washoe." Washoe had recognized herself and expressed the recognition linguistically.

The Gardners concluded that language was a capacity not unique to man. With this they challenged man's unequaled station in the universe and ignited interest in primate language studies. Soon Sarah, a young chimp under the supervision of David

Premack, learned to associate plastic chips of different shapes, sizes, and colors with over 130 specific words. Using the chips, she could produce questions, plurals, and negatives, and appeared to understand many other grammatical structures. She also understood cause and effect. When Premack showed Sarah a full apple and a cut apple and asked her how to get one from the other, Sarah chose the proper word—knife. She could also solve problems. When shown a videotape of a man trying to play an unplugged phonograph, she chose the right solution: to plug it in.

At Yerkes Regional Primate Research Center in Atlanta, Georgia, Duane Rumbaugh developed Yerkish, a linguistic system of geometric symbols displayed on a computer keyboard. His star chimp, Lana, became famous for her ability to press the appropriate buttons for "Please machine give Lana banana" and anything else she wanted.

More recently Rumbaugh concocted a test to see if two chimps could communicate with each other in Yerkish. Sherman and Austin were put in adjoining cages, each with a Yerkish computer panel. Sherman had the food, but it was locked in a box. Austin didn't know about the food, but he knew he had the key to the box—along with several other tools. After several requests to the human experimenter, Sherman concluded that he had to ask Austin for the key. He did—in Yerkish. Austin picked out the right tool and passed it to Sherman. Sherman opened the box and they shared the food.

Last but not least, Francine "Penny" Patterson has "talked" with Koko, a female gorilla, since 1972. The infant, named Hanabi-Ko (Japanese for fireworks-child), was born in the San Francisco Zoo on the Fourth of July, 1971. Six months later Koko was given to Penny and removed to a trailer on the Stanford University campus. Rapidly Koko began to learn sign language. Today she is proficient with over four hundred signs.

But Koko is not only bright (she measures between 85 and 95 on the Stanford-Binet Intelligence Scale, just below normal for a human being), she also has quite a personality—which she expresses through gestural language. For example, Koko is not averse to backseat driving. When they take the car out for a Sunday cruise she often signs to Penny to pull up at one of the numerous candy-vending machines she knows of on the Stanford campus. She likes games of pretend, like feeding her chimp dolly imaginary tea. She drew spiders after a sign language discussion about these insects and she signed "bad" after ripping up one of her toys.

Koko is also an adept linguistic liar. When she was caught poking a chopstick through a window screen she pretended to be smoking it. When asked what she was doing she signed: "I was smoking." She seems to understand past and future too. Three days after a biting incident she signed "sorry" to Penny. She also uses gestures with her new gorilla companion, Michael, like "Hurry up, get in here," and she often signs to herself at night when she looks through her picture books alone.

Like Washoe, Koko has made up new words. She calls a mask an "eye-hat," a Pinocchio doll an "elephant baby," a zebra a "white tiger." And she knows who she is. When Penny asks, "Are you an animal or a person?" Koko signs: "Fine animal, gorilla."

Until recently, Washoe, Sarah, Lana, Sherman, Austin, Koko, and other apes were believed to show the rudiments of human language. They all associated symbols with names for things; they were able to combine them to make two-word phrases; a few made up new words. But recently H. S. Terrace of Columbia University has created a nasty snag in primate language studies. He hadn't planned to. When Terrace first got his three-day-old chimp in 1973 he was determined to teach him sign language and he dreamed of the day he could ask the chimp (in Ameslan) about his thoughts, memories, moods, dreams, desires, and sex life. He even named the infant Nim (short for Neam) Chimpsky, after the linguist Noam Chomsky. Chomsky is known for maintaining that only human beings construct grammatical sentences, that this is the essence of language, that only man has language. Terrace hoped that Nim would prove him wrong.

Nim promptly made himself at home in a plush three-story town house on West Seventy-eighth Street in New York City. By his first birthday he had acquired the same number of sign words a human child uses at this age. And with time Nim began to make two-word sentences. Terrace eagerly videotaped all sessions in which the chimp responded linguistically. But slowly he came to an alarming conclusion. The chimp was mimicking his trainers. Often he produced the signs they wished him to—just by learning their subtle cues.

To Terrace, Nim's signing appeared uncomfortably similar to the behavior of a German circus horse, Clever Hans. At the turn of the century Hans made himself famous and his retired schoolteacher owner rich by spelling, reading, and solving math problems. For example, when asked, "What is two plus three?" he unhesitatingly stamped out "five" with a foreleg. But Hans was clever at only one thing: He knew human body language. When his questioner's body relaxed or when subtle changes were made in the questioner's eyes, head position, hands, or breathing, Hans knew to stop tapping—and though his trainer and audience participants were baffled and impressed, they had actually cued the horse to stop at the right answer.

Terrace believes that Nim, Washoe, Sarah, Lana, Koko, and all the other primates studied have learned to perform for their trainers through subtle cues of which the trainers are unaware. He points out that many of these apes' signs are simple repetitions, that they display no understanding of grammar, that no word sequences add new information, that they never make up novel phrases. Even Washoe's sign "water-bird," Terrace maintains, is two independent concepts, "water" and "bird," rather than a new combination. As he says: "You do not have a sentence just because you have a sequence of signs."

As his finale Terrace argues that most of the behavior attributed to Washoe and the others can be taught to pigeons. As proof he cites B. F. Skinner, the well-known behavioral psychologist from Harvard, who recently reproduced Sherman and Austin's cooperative communication with two white male pigeons, Jack and Jill. It took Jack and Jill three weeks to punch the correct color-coded buttons that enabled them to share their locked-up food.

The Gardners, Penny Patterson, and others are annoyed. They contend that because Nim had more than sixty trainers his performance was poor. They criticize Nim's teachers for using techniques likely to elicit imitative behavior. They say that Project Nim—which ended when Terrace ran out of money and Nim was four—was terminated too soon.

Everyone is upset. So is the definition and study of human language. Regardless of this mess, a few things are clear. Though apes do not produce any (or many) original sentences, or any complex grammatical constructions, they can associate about two hundred abstract gestures with things in their environment. They can refer to objects and events that are not present. They remember the past and project their thoughts into the future. And they communicate with us and among themselves with gestural words. Sarah even uses her head to solve problems. Washoe recognizes herself in the mirror. Koko lies. Not long ago it was thought that apes could do nothing but grimace, pant, and hoot.

It should not be surprising that Koko, Washoe, Nim, and other apes were able to acquire gestural symbols. Apes in the wild use gestures, postures, and facial expressions to communicate all the time. In fact, for them sounds are only a small portion of any social exchange. For example, a chimp may embellish his pant-hoot hello with a friendly slap on the hand, a pat on the fanny, or a big hug. An angry chimp compresses his lips and frowns as he is about to attack another. During a game of tag or tickle, a chimp puts on a play-face—with the upper lip drawn back to expose the upper teeth. And a chimpanzee equivalent of a human being's nervous smile is a closed grin, in which the lips are pulled back and the teeth are clenched but showing. These facial expressions, along with the appropriate body postures, social distances, and hand and arm gestures, accompany the whimpers, screams, squeaks, pants, coos, and giggles to help convey the animal's meaning. Often the sounds serve only to attract attention. Antics do the rest.

Gestures, postures, and facial expressions are a large part of human communication too. Facial expressions are the most informative—normally a dead giveaway to one's emotional state. In a recent experiment, trainee nurses were asked to lie about a series of films they had been shown. Because they were told that in their profession lying was sometimes important to reassure patients, the nurses were highly motivated to lie well. They were most conscious of their facial expressions, which the more skilled were able to control. All attempted to use fewer hand gestures, keeping their hands in their pockets or behind their backs at times they would normally use them to accentuate their vocal statements. Unconsciously, however, they touched their faces more often, concealing their mouths, tweaking their noses, or scratching their eyebrows at the moment of their lies.

Professional liars such as magicians, who know the importance of gestures, skillfully deceive their audiences with hands and body. The rest of us perform what Desmond Morris calls nonverbal leakage: We constantly give away our emotions through gesture, posture, and expression. In fact, words alone would never be convincing. Imagine saying "I love you" through tightly clenched teeth.

Because nonverbal communication is common to all people, and because it plays a tremendous role in the communication processes of the apes, it undoubtedly is an ancient form of human communication. So old, in fact, that Darwin was convinced that many complicated human emotions were expressed in the same gestural fashion by all human beings. To confirm this he sent a query to several colleagues around the world in 1867. He wished to know whether the natives of China, Australia, India, and North and South America expressed their emotions in the same way the English did.

He asked such questions as: "When a man is indignant or defiant does he frown, hold his body and head erect, square his shoulders and clench his fists?" and "Is disgust shown by the lower lip being turned down, the upper lip slightly raised, with a sudden expiration, something like incipient vomiting, or like something spit out of the mouth?" From the responses, and from his own work on facial expression and body posture, Darwin concluded that smiling, laughter, and feelings of embarrassment, indignation, disgust, guilt, pride, envy, contempt, jealousy, deceit, suspicion, vanity, humility, joy, sorrow, and many others were expressed the same way around the world; that they evolved in all human beings the same way physical characteristics did—as the result of selection and evolution. In 1872 he presented this view in "The Expression of the Emotions in Man and Animals."

Over one hundred years later Paul Ekman redid Darwin's experiment, traveling through Brazil, Chile, Argentina, the United States, Japan, and New Guinea with his camera. Ekman confirmed Darwin's hypothesis. Indeed, around the world people move their facial muscles and their bodies in the same way to express the same emotions. These gestures must have evolved long before man became modern.

Another way we communicate without using words is through intonation. For all other animals, this is an essential device. For example, Japanese monkeys make a cooing sound to express themselves. If high, smooth peaks are voiced at the beginning of a coo, the caller is simply informing others of his whereabouts so that group cohesion is maintained. These calls are calm and the caller is normally near but not in the mainstream of the group. When the high-frequency peaks are expressed late in the coo sound, however, the caller is excited. Normally he is looking for company, sex, or trying to appease a more dominant animal.

Intonation is so essential to animal communication, believes Eugene Moran, an ornithologist at the National Zoological Park in Washington, D.C., that he recently devised an electronic device that produces two-dimensional pictures of animal sounds. Then he compared the sounds of fifty-six species of birds and mammals from the wombat to the rhino. He found that all produced a low, harsh growl when angry and a high whine when frightened or friendly. He says that the configurations he picks up with his Sona-graph appear to be a universal animal language based on pitch and tone.

Humans use this tonal system too. Human Sona-graphs even look like those of wombats and the other animals Moran examined. Apparently we growl when we are angry, whine when we plead, and always raise our pitch when we say "I love you." Even very young infants can understand these changes in intonation.

Because posture, gesture, facial expression, and intonation are universal devices of animal and human communication, it seems safe to say that the protohominids forced from the trees between 14 million and 5 million years ago used them to chat among themselves. Maybe they had as many as sixty different calls. Like the gibbon, chimp, or vervet monkey, they uttered calls meaning "danger here," "come," "food," "let's be friends," "please gimme," "follow me," "I'm sorry," "drop dead," "I'm in pain," "I'm lost," "leopard near," and others. Each vocal statement was probably a specific series of sounds equivalent to a word. Perhaps they were capable of twelve separate sounds (or phonemes)—and all sixty calls were composed of these sounds. But, as with animal communication, the calls were never broken down into their component sounds and recombined. "Hoo-aa" always meant "danger"; "wraa-pa" always meant "figs." All calls were mutually exclusive.

They probably also used gestures. "Hello" was accompanied by smacking lips. "Goodbye" could well have been just a wave of the hand. And perhaps hundreds of facial expressions, hand motions, body positions, and vocal tones embellished vocal calls to provide an intricate system of interpersonal communication.

This "call system" probably served them very well when roaming the woodlands from one patch of trees to another. A few long-distance calls served to alert all in earshot about the location of food or a prowling leopard, or the whereabouts of an individual. All other communications would have been face-to-face affairs, where each protohominid easily expressed his feelings and desires through gesture, posture, vocal tone, and simple calls.

But all that was to change. Why? Because by the time bonded pairs were lying in each other's arms every morning, planning the day's activities, reviewing yesterday's, discussing their children or their debts, or describing distant places, you can be sure they needed more words.

Just think how much easier life would become once these savannah bedouins shared a few words for animals, plants, and places; a few terms for distance in space and time; a few numbers to describe the quantity of animals they had seen and a few terms for colors, sizes, shapes, and sounds. How easy life would be when everybody had a name, a simple way to ask a question, a diplomatic way to tell one another what to do. With a few environmental references, seasonal or rare foods could be located, dangerous areas could be avoided, and individuals could better express which plants to gather, which animals to hunt, where to meet, when, and by what route. This could make all the difference for a group of creatures dependent upon each other for survival.

Today there are over ten thousand works on the origin of language. Most of the authors speculate freely. Few agree. Even the most recently published 911-page scientific opus, entitled *The Origin and Evolution of Language and Speech*, concludes with the remark that theoretical differences are staggering: ". . . that the only consolation is that astronomy is in a worse mess."

No present scientific theory adequately explains how it came about that our ancestors first connected words with objects, then broke down their words into sounds and began to make new combinations of sounds into new words for other things. One popular theory is that language developed from gesture. According to this view, primitive man used gestures naturally—particularly when conversing at a distance. Gestures may have been used during the hunt, for the human voice is not built to scream, and noise would scare away the prey. So as hunting became more crucial to survival, particular gestures became associated with particular places, things, distances, relationships. These gestures were used first with the referent in sight, then back at camp when the referent was absent. Finally, because the gestures became too numerous and similar, certain noises became associated with particular gestures. With time, the noise, or word, took on the symbolic meaning of the place, animal, distance, or time—and the gesture was dropped.

Human beings still use gesture. We universally point at things and people—a gesture no other primate makes. We often use our hands in conversation, even on the telephone where the other party does not see them. The V sign with the first two fingers, the hand cupped behind the ear, the human smile, the clenched fist, the head shaken from side to side, and hundreds of other human gestures are employed around the world. One gestural advocate, Gordon Hewes, goes so far as to say that our light-skinned palms and soles—which are totally unlike the dark-skinned palms and soles of other primates—evolved to make human gestures visible to others during this early stage of human communication.

Perhaps some names for things evolved from gestures, but my guess is not many. Why? Because gesture is a multimodal system of communication requiring the gesturer to have free hands, the recipient to use his eyes. If you are carrying sticks, stones, children, and food all day, it would be impractical to use your hands to talk. And it would be impossible after dark—a good time to discuss plans and share experiences.

Hearing, through which we receive much nonwritten language today, seems the likely way that most information began to be passed in early man. This way the protohominids could listen while their hands and eyes were doing other things. Moreover, with the beginning of bipedalism, the mouth, tongue, and lips were set free to speak—they no longer were used to carry.

But most crucial to the beginning of human language was the

effect of bipedalism on the larynx, or voice box. In our four-footed (horizontal) relatives, the larynx lies directly behind the throat, making it impossible for them to articulate the many sounds we use in speech. But when early men and women rose onto their hind legs and began to walk, the larynx sank down the throat. With the larynx in this new position, the air emitted between the vocal cords travels a longer distance to the mouth. And during its travels up toward the lips, it is massaged by the undulating walls of the throat.

So with bipedalism, new, sophisticated sounds could be uttered. And if, as is likely, such sounds slowly became easier to articulate, easier to distinguish as well, then it is not too difficult to imagine a time, shortly after the protohominids had begun to walk erect and bond, when a male made a sound as he pointed at an antelope. His consort associated the sound with "antelope." And shortly the sound came to mean "antelope" among all the members of the band.

These associations probably were made over and over again. Sometimes a noisy child coined a word by babbling out an unusual sound as it shook an object. Or someone made a noise that sounded like an animal and, by onomatopoeia, it stuck. Perhaps someone found an egg and tried to imitate its shape with rounded lips—and out came a sound her companions came to associate with "egg." An excited spontaneous exclamation may have become the name of a unique event. Maybe a place where someone had an accident became associated with some characteristic sound that that individual made daily.

Nouns probably came first, because apes and young human children associate names with objects easily. Because human children are particularly drawn to words for objects that move, it seems sensible that early men out hunting would be, too— particularly when the objects were coming toward them. Then perhaps noises became associated with actions or processes— because children and apes learn these early too. For example, a noise uttered while killing, cutting, or smashing prey may well have become the word for kill, cut, or smash. And once verb associations were made they would have been particularly useful to protohominids working in groups who needed to direct one another's chores.

If studies of ape gestural language and human children learning language can further serve as models, then early men and women would have associated certain sounds with their intentions, too—like "I am going," "I want," "I am taking," and so on. They would have talked about the ways in which objects related to each other and to themselves—for example, an object's location, who owns it, what to do with it. Probably they also learned to make a distinction between "now" and "later." Koko the gorilla does this, and children learn it fast.

Though linguists are far from certain, the earliest words probably were those with an *m, n, p, b, g,* or *d* sound followed by the vowels *a* or *o*—for these are particularly easy for children around the world to reproduce. Undoubtedly early speakers used repetition, pitch, and intonation too. This way the same word—pronounced differently—could represent several places, objects, actions, or events.

But referential naming is not the "open" system of human language. Protohominid verbal communication was, in effect, an elaborate animal "call system" which became increasingly complex and flexible as it spread through groups and generations. Then, at some point, true human language came to be. Possibly a child invented it, for children tend to be less constrained by established practices. Perhaps it was invented many times, by many different individuals. Eventually, the new system stuck.

There are almost no speculations on how language "opened up." Among the few, however, is an intriguing one presented in 1964 by linguist Charles Hockett. It is known as the blending theory and—with my embellishment—it goes like this:

Among Lucy's grandchildren was a lazy boy. He had been a lazy toddler, always demanding to be carried, trailing behind the others on the march, and lounging around adults while the other children chased about. But he was a fast learner. He knew all the words for the plants his mother gathered. He could describe the places his parents took him in the summers and the names of everyone in the valley where they spent the winter months. Often he made up new words to describe what he saw around him. Many were met with disapproval. He was accused of babbling, of being a dreamy good-for-nothing kid. But a few of his new words had stuck. Particularly the

word *hoo-aa* he always used when he was scared. It had come to mean "danger" and everybody used it.

Now he was entering adolescence, however, and his mother and her sisters wondered if he would ever roam with the other boys, bring back meat, or leave the group to find a mate. Today he had gone off alone—a stupid thing to do—but he had mumbled "wraa-pa" before he left and his mother knew he was off to look for figs. As the fig trees were near the gully where they camped, she hadn't been worried for his safety.

But now it was getting late. The sun had sunk behind the mountains in the west. The group had begun to eat their evening vegetables, and his mother was annoyed. Finally she heard his footsteps coming along the pebbly path. He walked slowly, as usual, and as his silhouette appeared across the dried-up stream bed, she could see he was counting the figs that he had gathered. At least he has something to eat, she thought, as she wedged the last of her tuber into her mouth. Then she rose and greeted him with hunched shoulders, upturned palms, and an irritated frown. The message was clear—why are you late again? The boy replied, "Wraa-hoo," and settled down to pick the leaves and dirt away from the delicate fruit.

"Wraa-hoo?" Everyone was listening. This child had always been a problem and they wished to hear his explanation. But what did this new word mean? Everybody knew that *wraa-pa* meant "figs," that *hoo-aa* meant "danger." But the boy had not bothered to say either. Instead, he said only the first half of each and combined them into a single word. The older people shrugged and returned to their evening meal.

But the boy's younger sister didn't. She had listened to her brother's drivel for years and she realized that now he was simply saying "figs" and "danger"—both at once. She resolved not to go to the fig grove in the morning and when she whispered "wraa-hoo" to her girl friend, her sidekick resolved the same.

Words were breaking down. And through countless numbers of these blending "mistakes," the animal language of our ancestors gradually decomposed to become all those meaningless little noises we combine today to express ourselves linguistically. With time, rules of grammar would be added. Then, and only then, would our ancestors begin to use true human language.

It is no exaggeration to say that the "opening up" of human language was the single greatest achievement of our ancestors. Though human language surely arose from animal linguistic antecedents, as Darwin claimed, it certainly made man the unique creature he is today. As Descartes once said of us, ". . . none are so depraved and stupid, without even excepting idiots, that they cannot arrange different words together, forming of them a statement by which they make known their thoughts; while on the other hand, there is no animal, however perfect and fortunately circumstanced it may be, which can do the same."

We may never know exactly how man came to create language, or whether it was invented once or several times, but linguists like to speculate on when it probably occurred. The majority are conservative—placing the origin of language at only fifty thousand years ago. Among them is a specialist who has reconstructed the vocal tract of 100,000-year-old fossils and then, using a computer, established what sounds these individuals could have made. He maintains that due to the position and configuration of the voice box, these people were incapable of making many vowel noises; thus they were incapable of human language. Others disagree. They doubt the efficacy of his research. Furthermore, they maintain that one need not have the full complex of human sounds to have an "open" language. In this view, language could be much older than the conservatives believe.

This may very well be the case. It seems that human beings pick up language "naturally"—as if it were an instinct. They begin with coos and babbles in the first six months of life. By the age of two, normal children in every part of the world have broken down the complicated noises they hear around them from birth into the simple sounds of language. Once they have discovered the separate sounds, they begin to reassemble them as words. Nouns and verbs come first. Soon one-word sentences become two-word sentences and the most elementary rules of grammar are applied. Then they begin to refine their speech, adding new words and more complicated grammatical structures.

This they practice. Over and over, children "naturally" repeat what they have heard. And mother's baby talk helps. Adults around the world seem "naturally" to speak to their young in exaggerated, high-pitched tones and simple sentences. For good reason. The high, singsong pitch alerts the child to pay attention and the easy grammatical constructions are (remarkably) only slightly more advanced than the child's own grammatical ability. (Even adult laughing gulls simplify their calls to teach their young.)

Deaf children who are not exposed to oral or sign language make up a system of signs that is quite similar to natural spoken language. Apparently a deaf man in Micronesia (the first deaf man recorded in these islands) invented his own sign language and taught it to his friends so he could communicate with them. Even Genie, a thirteen-year-old "wild child" recently discovered in an attic in California where she had been locked since she was twenty months old, has since begun to use words and sentences.

Because children actively seek language, learn it the same way all over the world, and find it easy to learn, it is plausible that language acquisition is an innate biological process—and thus extremely old.

Probably the evolution of human language began when our first ancestors—the protohominids—started to bond. Because a bonded pair had to discuss their plans, they had to talk. With bipedalism they *could* talk. So, slowly, over millions of generations, individuals added new words to their vocabulary. As social life became more complex, their "call system" became more complex—then finally unmanageable. And words broke down into their component sounds—a few simple meaningless noises that early hominids began to combine and recombine to express their almost-human selves.

With a few extra tricks they would be men and women.

A FEW EXTRA
TRICKS

A poor degenerate from the ape,
Whose hands are four, whose tail's a limb,
I contemplate my flaccid shape
And know I may not rival him
Save with my mind.

—ALDOUS LEONARD HUXLEY
"First Philosopher's Song"

Anthropologists like to argue. And there is no larger, longer argument than that surrounding our human lineage. Rarely is there disagreement over the fossils associated with the proto-hominids. There are too few specimens, too few anthropologists willing to stick out their necks to deal with them. And no fossils have been found from the period between 8 million and 4 million years ago. So no one gets hot under the collar over nonexistent issues. After this blank period the first fossils to appear are Lucy and The First Family—living about 3.5 million years ago. As mentioned earlier, here the arguments begin. Don Johanson and others maintain that these specimens are the first of our ancestral line. Richard Leakey counters that they are just the beginning of a defunct line that never led to man. A few anthropologists take sides; most watch and waffle.

But when it comes to more recent fossils, those that represent individuals roaming the savannahs by 2 million years ago, every palaeontologist has an opinion. They began to argue in 1924 when miners blew up part of a limestone quarry in "The Place of the Lion," or Taung, South Africa. The explosion left visible the partial skull of what looked to the miners like a prehistoric ape, so they sent it to Raymond Dart, anatomy professor at the University of Witwaterstrand. To him it looked less like the face of an ape than that of an ancient human child. It had a human-looking jaw, somewhat human teeth, and a cranium (or brain-case) that was proportionately larger than any he had ever seen on any ape. Dart swore his Taung infant was on the threshold of humanity. And he reported this in the prestigious English journal *Nature* in 1925.

His colleagues—particularly the English—scorned Dart and his discovery. At that time the Piltdown hoax was in full swing,

175

and because this yet-to-be-exposed phony skull and jaw clearly showed that a large brain had evolved in tandem with an apelike jaw, the English were unwilling to accept the Taung infant. Furthermore, because Piltdown Man had come from English soil, the prevailing thought was that mankind had evolved in England—not Africa. So Dart was called inexperienced, his Taung infant an aberration. He coined his specimen *Australopithecus africanus* (meaning the southern ape of Africa).

But the English would eat their words. For in 1936 a young Scottish scientist, Robert Broom, found four partially complete skulls and several postcranial bones at Sterkfontein, South Africa. Here, in the open, rugged plateau country of the Transvaal region, the bones had been washed—or dragged by predators—into a deep cave behind an overhanging rock where they had sat for over 2 million years. When examined they looked like relatives of the Taung infant, with humanlike faces, small teeth, small bodies, and enlarged brains.

For a while Dart, Broom, and a few other palaeontologists believed we had descended from these hominids. But within the next ten years other fossils found in three new caves in the Transvaal region complicated matters. In Dart's cave at Makapansgat the fossils appeared similar to those at Taung and Sterkfontein. But in Broom's caves at Kromdraai and Swartkrans a larger creature came to light. His estimated weight was almost twice that of Dart's smaller *africanus* form, and though he also had an enlarged brain, he had huge teeth and a thick, heavy brutish-looking skull. They called him *Australopithecus robustus*.

With this the arguments began again. Which was our ancestor? Some said the smaller ones were females and the larger ones were males—both of the same species, both ancestors of modern man. Others felt that because of his huge teeth and giant heavy skull, *robustus* had spent his life eating only tough fruits and vegetables, while the small-toothed, gracile *africanus* had evolved to eating meat. Thus these South African specimens represented two entirely different species, it was reasoned, and it was *africanus* that had turned into man.

Palaeontologists remained stymied for ten years. Then, in August of 1959, Louis and Mary Leakey arrived at the Pan African Congress on Prehistory in today's Zaire. As reported by a colleague: "Louis was sitting in the bus holding on his knee a small square box and, by the expression on his face, it was obvious that he had something momentous to report." He had. He had found the skull of the first *East* African man—dated almost 2 million years ago. Mary had found it only a month earlier, while crawling over the dusty, layered sediments of Olduvai Gorge in the badlands of Tanzania. This Australopithecine was even more robust than those of South Africa and it came to be called *Australopithecus boisei*, after Charles Boise, an early sponsor of Leakey's work.

Then in 1961, with what is today called "Leakey's Luck," Louis found the partial skull of the creature whose whole skull would have measured almost 700 cubic centimeters. This is approximately 300 cubic centimeters larger than those of *africanus*, *robustus*, or *boisei*. And the individual lived at Olduvai 1.75 million years ago. Near the skull were hand bones, foot bones, a collarbone, and ten handmade tools.

The hand bones proved that this creature could press his thumb to his first finger in a peculiarly human fashion, which is necessary for making tools. The foot bones illustrated that this creature walked erect. And the tools lying in such close proximity appeared clearly to be those of this brainy hominid. Louis proudly called his specimen *Homo habilis*—or Handy Man—thus slotting him as our first real relative of the *Homo* line.

Now suddenly there were four creatures roaming around Africa and resembling us 2 million years ago. *Australopithecus africanus*, the gracile creature whose brain measured approximately 450 cubic centimeters and who lived in southern Africa; a larger, more brutish *Australopithecus robustus*, a contemporary in southern Africa who chewed predominantly tough vegetables and had an average brain capacity of 530 cubic centimeters; his even larger version *Australopithecus boisei* that Leakey found at Olduvai; the tall slim *Homo habilis*, also from Olduvai, whose brain measured 700 cubic centimeters. And to complicate matters, Leakey proclaimed that all varieties of *Australopithecus* —represented by hundreds of fossils—were those of a defunct stock of hominids. Only *Homo habilis* led to modern man.

He based his conviction on other evidence he had collected over the years from Olduvai Gorge. Two million years before, this area had been an emerald-colored lake nestled between four volcanoes that periodically showered it with lava, steam, and ash.

With wind and time the lake had dried up, then filled with layers of lake sediments and blowing sand. Finally, a seasonal river had cut through the sediment, leaving a three-hundred-foot-deep, twenty-five-mile-long gash in the earth's surface in Tanzania—a layer cake of history ready to be explored.

In 1931 Louis had made a bet that he would find evidence of early man in this dusty, desolate crevasse. That same year, on his first visit to the gorge, he had picked up a lava tool by the afternoon. Since then he had visited Olduvai almost seasonally, and periodically he had found an ancient tool that had served some former creature.

In the late 1950s he and Mary had begun to find more astonishing evidence of early man in Bed I, the bottom layer of the gorge. "Olduwan" pebble tools were everywhere. These are smooth stones the size of baseballs that primitive men and women had picked out of ancient streams and whacked with another rock to remove a couple of edges. The result was a crudely pointed chopper.

At one excavation site the Leakeys found a living floor, where almost 2 million years ago, hominids had butchered an elephant that had been trapped in a clay bog. They had left 123 of their tools around its broken bones. It seems these ancient butchers had been clever enough to drive the elephant into the bog. Near the bog Mary Leakey unearthed a pile of stones that had been deliberately arranged in a semicircle. Apparently these stones had served to secure piles of brush to make a lean-to almost 2 million years ago. Behind the lean-to early man had tossed his garbage— the remains of several meals and his worn-out tools.

Here, then, in Olduvai Bed I, was evidence of man's first home base, a butchering site where he snared, cut up, and shared a large animal with friends, leaving a plethora of his ancient tools as signatures of a time long gone. To the Leakeys these signs implied that by 2 million years ago some early hominids had a clear knowledge of the terrain, the animals in it, and an organized strategy of hunting them. Furthermore, they showed forethought in selecting the proper stone, and logic in shaping it into a tool that met with the fashion of the times. Last, these ancient people must have had the ability to explain to others how to make these tools, butcher an elephant, and build a lean-to—what appeared to be rudimentary language.

The problem with all these finds was that they convinced Louis that *Australopithecus boisei* was much too dumb to make tools and shelters, kill "big game" animals, and talk. Slowly he began to believe that none of the Australopithecines were our ancestors, but instead distant cousins destined to extinction; that these Bed I archaeological remains were left by brainier creatures. So Louis kept looking for the butchers who lived in the lean-to and made the tools. With a brain of almost 700 cubic centimeters, the new find, *Homo habilis*, had the mind for all this. Now finally, in Handy Man, Leakey thought he had found our true ancestor.

Many of Leakey's colleagues thought he was way off base. Leakey was a native of the Kenyan bush who cared little for convention. He was known as a flamboyant man and his colleagues were reluctant to discard several hundred fossils of *africanus*, *robustus*, and *boisei*, to replace them uncategorically with one skull of *Homo habilis*, and to dub this singleton man's first ancestor.

Besides, there was evidence that *boisei* and *habilis* had *both* frequented the emerald waters of Olduvai almost 2 million years ago, taking care to stay on the eastern edge where the salty marshes were fed by fresh water from the surrounding highlands. Both had camped near the game trails (now etched as depressions in the hardened clay) where ancient elephants, rhinos, horses, hippos, gazelles, and antelopes came to drink. Both had tramped through the reeds and papyrus at the swampy margins of the lake, avoiding crocodiles and hunting for catfish, waterbirds, snails, and slugs. And it seemed they both ate lizards, chameleons, rabbits, gerbils, bushpigs, birds, and anything they could catch on the savannah uplands that surrounded the lake and stretched toward the forested volcanic cones. So anthropologists were deadlocked—arguing the significance of *A. africanus*, *A. robustus*, *A. boisei*, and *Homo habilis*.

Time went on. In 1966, Leakey, F. Clark Howell (a longtime Leakey pal and fossil hunter), and others launched their first interdisciplinary research project (an idea of Leakey's) at a new site in southern Ethiopia. Here, between 2 million and 3 million years ago, a large river had flowed south from the Ethiopian highlands, dumping its fresh water, silt, and ash over a broad plain before it entered Lake Turkana in northwestern Kenya.

Along the river's edge had been meandering loops, stagnant swamps, marshes, mudflats, and riverine forests where today lie only dusty gullies and hardened rock escarpments beside the shrunken Omo River.

In the first season they unearthed a rich assortment of early hominids and their four-footed contemporaries. Mice, rats, squirrels, rabbits, mongooses, otters, and other small mammals had worked and played at the banks of the ancient Omo River. Apparently, extinct types of hartebeest, topi, gnu, koodoo, bushbuck, reedbuck, waterbuck, and impala had also come here to drink and die, leaving their bones at the water's edge. Along with them had drunk extinct types of horses, zebras, camels, pigs, giraffes, hyenas, monkeys—and early relatives of man.

Hominids of the *africanus* type were dated from almost 3 million years ago. *Boisei* began to roam the flats by 2.1 million years ago. And someone resembling Leakey's *Homo habilis* left his teeth and skull behind 1.8 million years ago. Some from among them, we know not which, suddenly began to make tiny tools of quartz at a quarry some twenty kilometers away and to carry them to the Omo River's edge about 2 million years ago.

Now, at Omo three of the four types of hominids had been found—an earlier *africanus*, a later *boisei*, and finally a big-brained *habilis*. No new clues. And palaeontologists continued to argue over who was our first ancestor. Then Louis's son, Richard, struck pay dirt at Lake Turkana.

Richard Erskine Leakey, middle son of Louis and Mary Leakey, spent most of his life—as his father did—in the African bush. By the time he was six he could recognize a fossil. As a child he heard anthropological jargon at the dinner table every night, and during the day his father sometimes sent him into the bush to scavenge and survive. He learned his "bushcraft" early.

By his teens the badlands of Olduvai were familiar turf to him and Richard spent many hours escorting visiting scientists around his parents' dig. Then, because he saw his father as a tyrannical, autocratic man, Richard entered the safari business to become independent. But this wouldn't last long. For in 1963, at age twenty, encouraged by his parents, he went off to investigate some curious deposits he had located in northern Tanzania. He found part of an *Australopithecus robustus*. That did it. Richard became an anthropologist.

But he had a lot of schooling to catch up on. He made up the last two years of high school in seven months and then passed his exams to enter university in England. He never went. Impatient to get back to fossil-hunting, he joined one of his father's research teams instead.

As he recalls: "I wanted to have my own show." And in 1968 his break came. That year he accompanied his father to Washington, D.C., where Louis was discussing his plans with his sponsor, the research committee of *National Geographic* magazine. When the business was over, Richard astonished all by mapping out his own plans for a new dig in a place he thought promising—Lake Turkana, just south of the Omo River in northwestern Kenya. Then he asked the sponsors to foot the bill. Agog, they did. But with this warning: "If you find nothing you are never to come begging at our door again."

Within weeks Richard was unpacking his equipment at his brand-new camp at Koobi Fora, a sunbaked spit of land on the parched eastern shore of Lake Turkana, a place known only to the flies, the crocodiles, passing herds of savannah beasts, and the local, not altogether friendly Shangilla tribesmen. In the first season he found beautifully preserved fossils of all kinds of animals but only three badly weathered *robustus* jaws. This was plenty for the *National Geographic* people, however, and the following year they financed an international team of geologists, palaeontologists, archaeologists, and others to excavate what would become the mother lode of fossil man.

Since then scores of Olduwan tools, dating perhaps as early as 1.9 million years ago, and well over three hundred separate fossil hominid bones have been found. Both the gracile and robust varieties of *Australopithecus* lived here. And so did an extremely controversial individual—hominid number 1470.

It was during the 1972 field season that a Kenyan member of the team found a few bits of bone weathering out of a sandy sedimentary layer in a steep gully near the lake's eastern shore. After careful sifting, over 150 more scraps were recovered and deposited in the lap of camp palaeontologist Meave Leakey, Richard's wife. Working as with a jigsaw puzzle—without the picture on the box and with many pieces missing—Meave and others began to put the skull together. Six weeks later they shaped the vacant head and face of a creature whose brain capacity was almost 800 cubic centimeters—double the volume of a chimpanzee's and more than half that of yours and mine. Furthermore, the skull was 2 million years old.

Suddenly a half century of scientific papers went down the drain—or so the Leakeys think. Since Dart found his Taung baby in 1924, anthropologists had firmly believed that *Australopithecus* was the first member of the human line. Decade after decade they spent poring over the crania and skeletal material of *Australopithecus africanus*, *robustus*, and *boisei*, measuring parts, comparing them with the bones of apes and modern man, dating them, and trying to establish their ranks in our evolutionary history. Only Louis Leakey doubted that *Australopithecus* was in our lineage, maintaining all his life that only the *Homo habilis* he uncovered at Olduvai was our ancestor. But where were his comrades?

Richard had found one. For hominid number 1470 (and another skull Richard found later) was a remarkably brainier character than *Australopithecus*, and he lived side by side with these small-brained forms at Lake Turkana 2 million years ago. Thus *Australopithecus* could have been a sideline destined for extinction, while 1470 and *Homo habilis* were already launched on the road to man.

After several years of bad blood between Louis and Richard, the old man flew to Koobi Fora to inspect the skull. They spent most of that night chatting and examining what Louis had always hoped he would someday find. Then, just three weeks later, the grand master of African palaeontology died.

Richard, like his father, feels that 1470 was the character who made the tools he has unearthed at Lake Turkana and butchered the hippo he excavated from the ancient shallows on the eastern shore. As he paints the scene of an afternoon 2 million years ago he sees a group of hairy *robustus* individuals sitting together on a grassy hillside above the lake, pulling up roots, stuffing them in their mouths, and chewing silently. They take care to stay near the trees, to which they will flee if necessary. Near them are some hairy *africanus* individuals that Leakey envisions sitting side by side, smashing nuts with rocks they have picked up to use but have not made into tools.

Below them both, on a spit of land near a deep lagoon where a freshwater stream meets the lake, Leakey sees some big-brained, hairless 1470s relaxing beside their sharpened digging sticks and containers made of animal skin or woven of grass. These early *Homo* are surrounded by nuts and an assortment of gerbils, rats, and mice they caught this morning. Suddenly a group of 1470-like males arrive carrying part of a pig they found and butchered on the plains. After a lot of chatter the meat is divided according to custom and tradition. And then, before the sun goes down, small family groups settle along their communal lean-to and share meat and vegetables while babbling, touching, and gesturing to express themselves in primitive human language.

Leakey avoids suggesting the nature of the family groups, and he mentions no sexual bonds of any type. But he makes it clear in his scenario that 1470 and his relatives were the *only* social, talking, sharing, home-based folks on the lake that day 2 million years ago; that the Australopithecines of both varieties simply sat by silently, ate alone, and watched.

But the argument over which of these creatures became modern man has not been solved. New dating techniques confirm that 1470 is 2 million years old—a time that corresponds well with *habilis* from Olduvai and with a skull found at Omo. Reexamination of the southern African fossils indicates that a tall, slender, big-brained character like *habilis* and 1470 lived at Sterkfontein and Swartkrans about this time. And a long-ignored skull from Java falls within the same time range and closely resembles these other forms.

All of these creatures had a cranial capacity of 600 to 800 cubic centimeters, larger than those of the Australopithecines, which measure 430 to 550 cubic centimeters. So, like his father, Richard Leakey is convinced that they alone represent the beginning of the human line. Their antecedents, he says, have not been found. Johanson disagrees. Though his fossil, Lucy, had a little brain, he quite understandably thinks that she and her friends—much earlier Australopithecines who lived and died some 3.5 million years ago—are in our line.

But the last bone isn't in. Right this minute Leakey, Johanson, and others are probably on their hands and knees, crawling (in the style introduced by the Grand Old Man himself) over the rugged, barren moonscapes of Kenya, Tanzania, Ethiopia, Pakistan, and perhaps Arabia. They all want to find something from the earlier deposits between 8 million and 4 million years ago—

the mystery time from which no fossil has yet been found. They want to fill in the gap between those elusive protohominids—the missing link—and the later fossils, Lucy, 1470, and *Homo habilis*.

But regardless of what they find, it is clear that by 2 million years ago our ancestors, whatever lineage you wish to believe in, had acquired a few extra tricks. Someone was making tools. At Olduvai they were making predominantly big choppers that they probably used to smash nuts or bones. But they used smaller discoidal chunks and polyhedrons too—maybe to hurl at the temple of an exhausted animal they had tracked all day. And they had begun to pick up the slivers (or flakes) they had whacked off of larger rocks to use for cutting meat and scraping skins. At Omo, early people had found a quartz quarry in the hills above the river. Here they had made small crystalline tools which they then carted to the water's rim to use on game. Just south of there, someone else was making tools at Lake Turkana, and a new 1981 report cites the finding of these tools beside a small stream in the Hadar region of Ethiopia. They are the oldest ever found—dating almost 2.7 million years ago.

In each area the tools resembled each other. When one man or woman at Olduvai made a chopper, another copied the technique, and the finished product looked the same. So in each area fathers were teaching sons, mothers were teaching daughters, and tool traditions were being passed from one generation to the next. Local fads had begun.

Two million years ago people were killing big game animals. At Olduvai they killed an elephant, at Lake Turkana, a hippo. These animals were bigger, stronger, faster, and fiercer than the hominids were. So they had to hunt, trap, or snare them, drive them into bogs, or wound them and chase them down. Then they had to cut up and divide the parts. So someone had learned to cooperate, to organize, to share.

Someone was building shelters too. Even the brilliant chimpanzees sit in the rain with their hands over their heads and miserably endure a rainy day. But by 2 million years ago someone at Olduvai had the sense to shelter himself and others from the elements.

Making tools, killing big animals, and building homes required brains. And by 2 million years ago *all* the individuals who roamed the hills, slept in the gullies, and congregated at the lakes and streams in Africa were sporting larger skulls and bigger brains than their predecessors. Here was our greatest extra trick.

To make sure that the human brain had begun to sprout, Heinz Stephan and others at the Max Planck Institute for Brain Research in Frankfurt, Germany, devised a progression index for all mammalian brains in which the size of the mammal's brain was measured against that of a standard animal—in this case a tree shrew, a tiny, rat-sized primate. In this index, *Homo sapiens* brains measured on the average of 29. Chimp brains measured 12. The smallest Australopithecine skulls measured 21—within the human range.

But far more important than simple brain enlargement is the reorganization of the brain, and it is likely that this also had begun by 2 million years ago. Or so thinks Ralph Holloway. For years Holloway has cluttered the anthropology lab of Columbia University with endocasts—the rubber latex casts of the insides of modern and fossil skulls. These lumpy blobs of rubber reveal the contours of the brain.

A lot can be surmised from the surface of the brain. For example, the visual lobe in the back of the brain is divided from the thinking lobe at the top of the brain by a seam. This groove can be seen in Holloway's endocasts. In the brains of apes and monkeys this groove runs anterior to the same groove in the brain of modern man. Thus, in modern man the thinking area has expanded and the visual lobe has decreased in size. Holloway's endocasts of early *Homo* and *Australopithecus* skulls show this groove in the same position as in modern man— indicating that by then this part of the brain had begun to expand for more complicated thinking.

These rubber blobs show another thing too—the beginning of human language. But what is it in our brains that gives us the connection between a nonsense sound and a complicated feeling, that provides us all with an innate sense of grammar, that drives us to perceive the world through language? Several little bulges. And Holloway found that one of them had begun to sprout in the famous 1470 skull, as well as in a robust Australopithecine skull from South Africa. To appreciate the incredible implications of Holloway's find you must know a little more about your brain.

The human brain is quite a gadget. It has an average volume of

1,400 cubic centimeters. This is over three times larger than a chimp's brain of 400 cubic centimeters and almost three times larger than the gorilla brain of 500 cubic centimeters. It weighs about three pounds and looks the size of a small canteloupe. Relative to body mass it is the largest among living creatures. The dolphin's brain comes next.

In the human brain are about 20 billion little neurons, or nerve cells, each of which transmits electrical currents to between 1,000 and 100,000 neurons in its vicinity. Thus the number of different pathways a current can take is, as Carl Sagan says, ". . . far greater, for example, than the total number of elementary particles (electrons and protons) in the entire universe."

Many of these neurons lie in the deepest, most primitive part of the brain—tissues that surround the final bulb at the end of the spinal cord. As Paul MacLean, the head of the Laboratory of Brain Evolution and Behavior of the National Institute of Mental Health, sees it, neurons in this part of the brain govern instinctual behaviors such as territoriality, aggression, ritual, and the establishment of social hierarchies. He calls it the reptilian brain because these creatures seem to depend on it to survive. He is not averse to saying, however, that we use this part of the brain also—particularly in committee meetings where strutting, preening, showing off, and status duels predominate.

Above and surrounding the reptilian brain are a group of structures in the middle of your head known collectively as the limbic system. Neurons in these areas, MacLean claims, govern your emotions and impressions. When you are overcome with joy, paralyzed with fear, struck by love, stoned on LSD, or in spiritual ecstasy, it is neurons in the limbic system that are doing electrical dances.

Like the reptilian part of the brain, the limbic area is old (at least 150 million years old), and it is thought that all animals, except man, use it to express themselves linguistically. Thus caws, squawks, bowwows, meows, hoots, and other animal sounds are almost totally emotional. (Even human beings whose more sophisticated language centers have been destroyed revert to the limbic system to communicate. Their utterances consist solely of swear words and emphatic "yes" and "no" responses.)

Finally, above and surrounding the limbic system is the cortex, the gray, convoluted mass of spongy material that lies directly below the skull. In man the cortex is divided into two asymmetrical hemispheres, the right and left, connected by a mass of nerves. It is actually two quite different brains, each with different functions. Thus, if you are right-handed, your right hemisphere is your artistic brain, while your left hemisphere is your brain for language.

In the left brain lie two extraordinary masses of cortical material, Broca's area and Wernicke's area—named after the men who discovered them. These masses are located approximately above the left ear and are divided from each other by a deep cortical seam. Anterior to this fissure is Broca's area, the area that seems to direct the mouth, tongue, throat, and vocal cords to produce speech sounds. It is this area that Holloway's endocasts show had begun to sprout 2 million years ago.

Behind Broca's area and separated by the seam is Wernicke's area, which seems to provide the ability to understand spoken words. Posterior to both areas is an association area, a lump of cortical tissue that acts as a "way station" between the senses and linguistic noise. This tissue integrates the word *cow* with the fat, placid, smelly creature that goes "moo." If Broca's area had begun to expand in the creatures that roamed the Transvaal, Olduvai, the Omo River basin, and Lake Turkana 2 million years ago, then these other linguistic areas were probably also beginning to expand.

And herein lie the incredible implications of Holloway's endocasts. If indeed these blobs of rubber, the interiors of ancient skulls, indicate that some areas of language had begun to grow in the cortexes of our ancestors by 2 million years ago, then these people had begun to use their cortexes to talk. Thus they were finally freed of the limbic system, the time-honored linguistic center of all other creatures. Now emotional conversation could be circumvented, enabling an entirely new kind of communication—abstract thought.

What a remarkable achievement. Millions of years before, protohominid males and females had begun to bond. And through an elaborate chain of social consequences they had now begun to evolve language centers in their brains. With cortical language they could discuss, plan, organize, report, instruct, command, theorize, joke—to produce millions of nonemotional statements about their world. Furthermore, language permitted them to conceal their feelings—in fact to lie with eloquence and ease. This ability could have been of tremendous social value when people in small groups had to get along.

With language, man could improve his technology, begin his religions and governments, and pass his traditions down to us.

Soon our ancestors would populate, then dominate the earth.

OUR GANG

O brave new world,
That has such people in't!

   —WILLIAM SHAKESPEARE
    The Tempest

The sun had not risen over the hills behind him, and he stood in the shadow and the quiet one and a half million years ago. He looked around carefully. Before him, in the shallows of the lake, the reeds were long and still. A group of hippos were blissfully chewing the tender spring shoots. Water bugs tracked the surface of the water, leaving brief impressions of their early morning search for food. Below them in the mud, tiny crabs moved effortlessly through their miniature universe around his feet—which were firmly planted in the swamp.

Around the lake the fig trees and acacia trees rose above the underbrush and spread like fingers through the delta plain. In one tree on the far shore a group of monkeys had come to feed, and their chatter drifted across the lake. This was good. His friends—apparently unnoticed—were hiding in the bushes beneath the monkeys' breakfast spot. No pigs had been disturbed in the underbrush that hugged the water's edge. No waterbucks had shuffled from their nighttime nests below the trees. No birds had called to others announcing the intruders.

The moment had come. He lifted both arms above his head to signal his companions. Then firmly he raised his foot and splashed it down before him—sinking deep into the mud. Then another forceful step. And another and another. The water bugs took nosedives in the waves. The crabs fled noiselessly below. The hippos stopped chewing and raised their heads to survey the menace to their morning calm.

Brown eyes met brown eyes, both man and hippo motionless. Then the mud-caked hippos moved away, farther into the lake, to resume their grazing. Once again the big human feet shattered the surface of the water. The man was moving closer, rippling the water and disturbing their peaceful morn-

191

ing meal. Again the hippos withdrew—now closer to the distant shore.

Suddenly, out from their ambush in the bushes, six men dashed into the muddy lake. The monkeys screeched. The birds took flight from the shrubs. And the hippos plunged toward the land. A baby hippo had been singled out, and as its mother lunged for freedom the hunters separated the infant from the group. Then one perfect shot. A fist-sized rock struck the infant on the temple.

In 1979 Kay Behrensmeyer dug up the hunter's tracks— preserved footprints of a man who had splashed through Lake Turkana of western Kenya tracking hippos 1.5 million years ago. He had stood about five and a half feet tall and weighed about 120 pounds. He had a human body, slightly shorter and stockier than those of modern people. But he had a human brain.

Richard Leakey had found his skull on the same lake. It measured 850 cubic centimeters (almost within the range of modern man's of 1,000 to 2,000 cubic centimeters), and though this creature had a small face, thick browridges that jutted out above his eyes, large teeth, and thick bones in the back of his head to support his bulging shoulder muscles, he could well have passed at a Halloween party today if he had worn a mask. So it was soon reported that Leakey's skull and Behrensmeyer's footprints were the remains of *Homo erectus*—the first unquestionable member of the human line.

At Olduvai Gorge *erectus* left his tools. Apparently about a million years ago the weather in the gorge turned cool and dry. As the ancient lake dried up, the first hominid inhabitants had departed. A layer of sterile sand soon covered their camp of stones and their crude Olduwan pebble tools. Then, many centuries later, with a climate change to warmer, wetter days and nights, the lake bed became a stream, and new inhabitants, evolved *Homo erectus* people, arrived. Here they camped and left behind big hand axes.

These tools were considerably fancier than the Olduwan pebble tools of their predecessors. Formerly, hominids had whacked off only one or two edges of a water-worn pebble to achieve a sharpened edge. Now *Homo erectus* was carefully chipping off edges on all sides to make long, almond-shaped and pear-shaped tools. Moreover, when *Homo erectus* knocked off a big flake, he often used the flake, too, evening its sides, sharpening its point, and rounding its butt end for efficient use. The big tools he used for chopping, pounding, or crushing; the smaller, more delicate tools for boring, scraping, or carving. And every available hard material was used. He made large, sturdy tools of lava, quartzite, and chert, and smaller tools of quartz and bone.

At the gorge, Mary Leakey found 434 artifacts in all. And in 1950 she found their maker—over two hundred fragments of a skull she collected in a dusty gully. After carefully reconstructing the parts—done on odd Sundays, as she recalls—Mary Leakey found herself staring into the vacant skull cap of a *Homo erectus* with a brain capacity of over 1,000 cubic centimeters. This person had camped beside the stream at Olduvai a million years ago. And that he had made these fancy hand axes became certain when she later unearthed a cranium, femur, and pelvic bone of a slightly more recent *Homo erectus*—dated 700,000 years ago— lying right next to similar tools.

But no mysteries shroud the life of *Homo erectus*. No one sports skinned knees or aching backs from crawling over the barrens of the ancient world to find his remains. No one spins long theories about his ability to walk, make tools, or hunt. For these tools, known as Acheulean tools—after the site of their first discovery near St. Acheul, France—are found not just in France and at Olduvai, but at *Homo erectus* sites on the grass- lands of southern Africa, the sand dunes of Algeria, the tundras of Spain, the plains of Hungary, and the steppes of Russia. To the east, in Burma, China, and Indonesia, *Homo erectus* left simpler tools resembling the former Olduwan tradition. With the exception of the older *Homo erectus* finds at Lake Turkana, all dated between one million and a half million years ago.

Because the bones and tools of *Homo erectus* have been found along stream banks, channel bars, swamp margins, and lake shores, near springs and in caves from northern China to southern Africa, there is no doubt that by a million years ago *Homo erectus* had successfully migrated from his cradle in the African tropics. Why he left, we do not know. Probably because he had to.

Fleet had left camp early that morning, followed a game trail up the steep cliff, and crawled through thorny bushes to a small clearing under an overhanging rock. Here a few last chunks of quartzite jutted from a seam below the crumbly cliff, and with time and muscle power he extracted one. Then he sat and struck it with a stone—whacking off slivers on all its sides until a perfect hand ax emerged. It was shaped like a giant flattened teardrop with a rough blunt end and a tapered piercing point.

He planned to use it soon. Maybe to chop the tough meat from the shoulder of a rhino, to carve the tender fillet from near its spine, or to smash its skull to extract the fatty brain. He sat, fingering the ax, and speculated on the kill to come.

But the sun was high and there was much to do back at camp. So he picked up the bladelike slices he had just whacked from his new weapon, counted them, and piled his quartzite tool, the slivers, and some berries he had collected into his buckskin pouch. Then he knelt and crawled out from the quarry. Before he left, however, he stood and looked around. He knew he would not be back.

It was an easy walk down to the river and he enjoyed every step. He had made the last of the tools he needed, and tomorrow he and his family would be heading north.

This was something new. For days Fleet had sat with his wife, her sister, and her sister's husband discussing the situation. They all agreed they loved this land. They knew the streams where the bushbuck lingered, the springs where the zebras, giraffes, and elephants could be ambushed. They knew the cliffs where they could stage nighttime raids on the sleeping baboons. Moreover, they knew every patch of yarrow, every stand of chives, and every bee tree. Regularly they checked the buds, shoots, and berries, so they could easily predict which would be abundant and when to return to collect them.

But so could everyone else. Often their campsites, water holes, ambush spots, quarry sites, and berry patches were crowded when Fleet and his family arrived. People were multiplying. And with the establishment of home bases and the evolution of cooperation millions of years before, the sick and injured could stay in camp. Sprained ankles and fevers had changed from fatal diseases to minor ailments. As a result, Fleet and his relatives lived longer.

This was fine. His wife's father could remember distant places he had roamed as a child and the habits of certain animals rarely seen. This knowledge had been helpful in lean years. His wife's aging mother was a great help with the children. So he had brought them meat, given them the pelts of antelopes he killed, and listened to their stories.

The group had grown too large, however. Often discussions had turned into bitter arguments and Fleet spent too much time providing for his in-laws' needs. Finally he had persuaded his wife, her older sister and her husband—a man whom Fleet admired for his deadeye aim—to split off from their kin, take their children, and move north, following the game to unfamiliar territory. Here they hoped to find new camps, new quarries, new water holes, new ambush spots, new cashew groves, new berry patches and bee trees. And if all went well, they planned to return, and to encourage others to join them in the north.

Homo erectus began to venture north from Africa in small family groups—moving perhaps no more than thirty miles during each generation. At this rate they would have expanded from Olduvai through Arabia to Turkey and over the Dardanelles to southeastern France in less than five thousand years. Moving only ten miles per generation from East Africa, they would have reached Peking in twenty thousand years. But there was a second reason *Homo erectus* people began to migrate out of Africa—they could.

By 1 million years ago the earth had undergone another tremendous drop in temperature. No one knows exactly why this occurred but bright ideas aren't lacking: It may have had to do with solar radiation, solar particle emission, sunspot activity, volcanic action, ocean circulation, or minute changes in the earth's axis and orbit. Whatever the fundamental cause, the glacial ages began.

As the temperature fell, snow piled in the high country of northern Europe, Asia, and North America. With cooler summer weather, less snow melted. So year after year, century upon century, mile-high crusts of ice began to form. Gravity forced them to move down from the mountain peaks, carving out valleys, pushing before them boulders, trees, sand, and dirt, and extending the chilly weather to the south.

Each cold spasm was intense, lasting several thousand years. Then a warmer interglacial period occurred and the frightful weather eased. As snows melted and the glaciers retreated to the north, torrents of water poured onto the thawing land. (In fact, we are in an interglacial period today and should expect the beginning of another glacial age in the next few thousand years.) But during these long, cold spasms, glaciers locked much of the oceans' water in ice. The sea level dropped over four hundred feet during each glacial age and left wide land pathways to the north. By a million years ago, *Home erectus* could travel along these highways.

Furthermore, a new ecological niche developed in the cool northern latitudes. Where pines, spruce, firs, willow, birch, and elms had once stood near lakes and streams that spotted the savannahs of Eurasia, now treeless tundra dominated the northern climes. Here the land was locked in permafrost—a boggy swamp in summer, a bitter, barren wasteland during the long winter months.

In the summer the woolly mammoth, woolly rhino, wild horse, giant elk, wolf, and many others ventured to these northern tundras to thrive and multiply in the cool summer weather of 50 to 54 degrees Fahrenheit. Then, when the cloudy, windy days turned harsh, they headed south to slightly warmer grassland and woodland areas in what is now southern Europe, the Middle East, and central Asia. Here they joined the fox, lynx, wildcat, wolverine, cave hyena, and cave lion who prowled the meadows looking for lemmings, marmots, and other animals that nested in the cool high grass. Where the pines, birch, and willows grew thickly, deer grazed beneath the trees. Brown bears fished the streams and beavers dammed the ponds. For thousands of years these species and many others proliferated in the forests and tundras of Eurasia. And, with the exception of those that became extinct in modern times, they evolved into many of the animal forms we know today.

By a million years ago, glaciers had also accumulated on the high volcanic peaks of East Africa, and below them the land was often cooler all year long. Sometimes torrential downpours, sometimes unusually long dry seasons, reflected the major changes occurring in the north.

So the unpredictable weather and increasing competition for space encouraged *Homo erectus* to roam from his birthplace in the tropics. The broad land bridges enabled him to move north. And the abundant large game animals he encountered enticed him to spread deep into Eurasia.

The first *Homo erectus* bones ever found were unearthed in Java almost a century ago. In 1892 a young Dutch anatomist, Eugene Dubois, came to dig along the terraces of the steamy Solo River, and that same year he found part of an ancient skull and thighbone (the femur). They were dated to 750,000 years ago. Although the browridges on the skull were thick and protruded above the vacant sockets of ancient eyes, this creature's cranial capacity measured 850 cubic centimeters. And his thighbone, Dubois established, was completely modern. So Dubois hailed his fossils as an ancient ancestor of man.

At the time, anthropologists were skeptical. They were reluctant to associate a modern femur with such a primitive head. So a few identified the find as a modern microcephalic idiot. Others called it a giant gibbon. Some accepted it as an ancient human being. Of course, no one was sure. But in the 1920s Peking Man was found. This spectacular cache of *Homo erectus* bones was unearthed at Choukoutien, or Dragon Bone Hill, just thirty miles from Peking in northern China.

For centuries the Chinese had been roaming the mountain gorges, hills, gullies, and caves of Mongolia and China looking for ancient bones. Although time after time the expeditions had returned successful, the fossil hunters sold their specimens at the doors of Chinese chemists and apothecaries. These precious artifacts were ground into fine, sour-tasting powders that the Chinese swallowed as elixirs to cure minor ailments.

Hearing of these expeditions, Davidson Black, a Canadian professor of anatomy at Peking University Medical College, launched his own in 1927 and discovered a lower molar of peculiarly human shape in a large, debris-filled limestone cave— Choukoutien. With this, excavation began. During the next ten years, 14 skulls, over 150 teeth, and the remains of more than 40 individuals were unearthed. Their limbs were modern, and though their skulls were brutish they measured between 850 and 1,300 cubic centimeters—well within the range of modern man.

Curiously, the bones of many individuals were charred—as if they had been roasted. Others had been smashed to extract the marrow. Some of the skulls had enlarged holes at their bases— evidence that someone had devoured the brains of these *Homo erectus* individuals. And whoever did it left tools behind— chopping tools that *Homo erectus* was then using in northern China. Here, for the first time, was evidence of cannibalism.

Possibly these ancient cannibals had dined on deceased friends, the way traditional New Guinea tribesmen sometimes do to gain the power of a beloved dead relative. More likely there had been a bloody battle, perhaps over who was to occupy Dragon Bone Hill in the dead of bitter winter or in the early spring when the elephants lumbered past their doorstep going north. The losers had been killed, roasted, and eaten.

Though these ancient *Homo erectus* cannibals left behind the first evidence of man's inhumanity to man, they also left behind the first sign of complicated culture—fire. Within the pile of bones were traces of hearths, campfires at which early inhabitants of the Chinese tundra warmed their hands and roasted enemies more than 750,000 years ago.

The controlled use of fire was an epochal development. For millions of years ancient people must have fled their homes in Africa when volcanoes disgorged balls of fire, or when lightning struck and flames swept across the plains. Undoubtedly they picked their way back home as the embers finally paled. Perhaps they found that the slain pig they had deserted the night before was wonderfully tender and tasty after it had been naturally roasted. Perhaps some fires near oil seepages burned for several months and people learned that to sleep near the flames protected them from prowling beasts. Occasionally an ingenious individual may have learned that he or she could carry embers in a baboon skull, or wrapped in moistened leaves, and that blowing gently on them later in the day would revive the flame.

Human beings are mesmerized by fire. The smell of burning wood, the crackling sound and flickering, flashing light can put us in a trance. Even our distant relatives of Southeast Asia, the tarsiers—little nocturnal primates with huge eyes and suction cups on some of their dainty fingertips—are attracted to the firesides of Indonesian villagers. They steal in unnoticed, grab the burning coals, and disappear into the night. So it seems reasonable that our ancestors began to play with fire long ago.

But in Africa they didn't need fire to survive. As people moved north, however, where the summer nights were cool and the winter months a horror, they began to need fire to survive. So, through trial and error, chance and circumstance, *Homo erectus* learned to control flame.

What a change this would make. Now the fireside could become an institution, a cohesive force, a place to dance and tell stories late at night. But that's not all *Homo erectus* must have done with fire. Perhaps people used the fire to harden wood for better spears. Probably they carried torches to drive herds of bison, elephants, and horses toward their lethal hunting snares. They must have thrown the embers at the yellow eyes of ancient saber-toothed tigers and hyenas whose cave homes they had usurped. And surely they huddled around the flames and slept securely within the halo of protective light.

Now, for the first time in history, men and women were no longer children of the sun. No longer would they have to get up at dawn and use the precious daylight hours to make their tools, hunt for meat, and divide the spoils. No longer bound by the circadian rhythm of all other animals, they had finally won a unique place for man.

The bones of Peking Man stirred the scientific world. Our immediate ancestors had been found, and those who had doubted Dubois's Java fossils abruptly changed their minds. By then, however, Dubois had become an embittered, eccentric old man. He thought that the Choukoutien specimens were part of a master plot, elaborately staged by his colleagues to prove him wrong. So he went into permanent hiding and buried his Javanese skull and thighbone in a chest beneath the floorboards of his dining room.

A worse fate befell the bones unearthed at Choukoutien. As one story has it, they were packed in crates to accompany the luggage of a young United States Marine Corps doctor bound for home in 1941. With the beginning of World War II the doctor was imprisoned by the Japanese troops then in control of northern China. Apparently he left the crates with Chinese friends, but they were never seen again. Perhaps the bones were eventually ground up into powder and sold as elixirs for belly-aches. More likely, as another theory goes, they were shipped to America on a freighter that sank in the South China Sea.

There is still a $150,000 reward for the missing material, and the tale continues. As recently as January 1981, *The New York Times* reported the story of a Chicago financier who raised $640,000—allegedly to search for the missing bones and make a film about Peking Man. Neither film nor bones have been produced and the money has disappeared. Probably these bones of Peking Man are gone for good. Luckily, however, good plaster casts exist of many of the skulls—the only remains of this remarkable cache at Choukoutien.

But *Homo erectus* has left his hearths elsewhere. The first European site was found in 1960 when workmen were dynamiting to lay a road in the valley of the Durance River not far from Marseille, France. By accident they exposed the back chambers of a long-buried cave, and when archaeologists began to dig they discovered traces of charcoal, ash, and fire-cracked stones in five reddened hearths dated a million years ago. In a deep cave on Katsika, or Goat Mountain, near the tiny village of Petralona in Greece, the remnants of burned animal bones trace fire in this area to 700,000 years ago. And in sediment near the charred animal bones, encased in a stalagmite, was the skull of an early European man.

By far the most spectacular site of fire and the life of *Homo erectus*, however, comes from a valley in north central Spain near a village called Torralba. Some 400,000 years ago this broad, steep-sided valley lay, as it does today, as a low pass through the mountains, connecting plateaus to the south and north. The weather then was cooler than now, with July temperatures of 57 degrees Fahrenheit and January temperatures of 25.

To the north of the valley lay the cool, windswept tundras just below the glaciers' edge. To the south lay warmer woodland and grassland areas. Annually the woolly mammoths, woolly rhinos, primitive horses, wild oxen, several types of deer, and predators such as the lion and wolf migrated from south to north and back again.

Above the valley on the ridges and plateaus, pine trees thrived. Here there was little surface water, for the area was made of limestone, and water from autumn rains and winter snows percolated deep into the rock. On the valley bottom, however, this water gushed out as springs, and in the springtime it formed a sluggish meandering stream amid miles of sedge and swamp.

To this valley *Homo erectus* came annually, or perhaps twice a year, to kill young elephants. As many as four or five family groups (about a hundred people) camped on the ridges, watched the animals below, planned their hunt, and then, when the time was right, descended to execute their kills. They left behind the remains of over thirty elephants, twenty-five primitive horses, twenty-five red deer, ten oxen, and six rhinos—all uncovered on the valley floor.

How did they trap these beasts? Apparently with fire. The excavator, F. Clark Howell of the University of California at Berkeley, found bits of charcoal and carbon scattered in several spots throughout the valley. To him these did not look like hearths, where charcoal and fire-cracked stones are often concentrated, but like the last remains of tiny brush fires that *Homo erectus* set to drive his prey to areas where they would be mired in the mud. Then, because large rocks lay near the skeletons of the fallen beasts, it seems that the hunters descended and stoned the confused animals to death.

After the kill had been made, the hunters apparently settled down to butcher the meat. They pierced the tough skin of young mammoths with flint and limestone axes, then cut through the ten centimeters of fat with heavy, diamond-shaped quartzite cleavers. These they left behind near their prey. Finally, after they had severed the ligaments and parceled out the giant pieces, it seems that tiny family groups departed to nearby spots to divide their spoils, because delicately shaped scrapers, blades, and pointed flakes were left in scattered clumps beyond the larger butchering sites. In all, over two thousand tools, both big and small, and countless pieces of smashed-up fossil animal bones have been recovered from the valley floor.

But where did Torralba Man live? No campsites have been found. Perhaps they slept on the ridges above the valley, and their property has long since crumbled down the steep cliffs. One clue comes from Ambrona, a second site just two miles down the valley, where another massive slaughter has been unearthed. Here again, about 400,000 years ago, *Homo erectus* people had butchered forty to fifty elephants, several horses, red deer, and wild oxen. Scattered clusters of charcoal indicate that here, too, they had deliberately set fires to drive the game into the muck. And, just as at Torralba, clumps of larger tools lay near where the fallen prey had been dismembered, and piles of small tools showed where the finer butchering was done.

At Ambrona, however, a single elephant skull lay on one excavated floor. Near the skull were several elephant bones which had been carefully arranged in a twenty-foot-long line. Close by was a four-foot tusk which had been whittled on the tip to make a sharpened point. It looked as if someone had thrust the tusk into the ground, thrown hides over it to make a roof, and anchored the hides to the ground with the elephant skull and line of bones. Here were the remains of a distinctly human shelter.

Many more homes were found at Terra Amata, a site near Nice in southern France which is dated at the same time-period as Ambrona and Torralba. Apparently a band of ancient hunters came here to camp near the mouth of a small river. Judging from their fossilized fecal matter (coprolites), which contained young seeds, they had come in early spring. Here they constructed oval huts, the largest fifty feet long and eighteen feet wide. Each was made of sturdy interlocking branches, supported by posts driven into the ground and secured with rocks.

It seems that Terra Amata Man entered his dwelling at one end and sat around his fire below the smoke hole in the center. Several hand-carved limestone chopping blocks seem to indicate that he smashed bones of elephants, wild boars, deer, and other animals beside his hearth. Then he cooked his meat and reclined around his fire to eat, to suck the marrow from the bones, and to talk away the evening in the firelight.

These remnants of early European man call forth several provocative questions. At Torralba, after one of the elephants had been butchered, part of its left side had been reconstructed and the bones carefully replaced in the mud. Was this a game or ritual? Also at Torralba waterlogged bits of pine showed marks of polishing, whittling, bored holes, and cutting scars. Were these parts of spears or good luck charms? And what happened to the skulls of the elephants that Torralba and Ambrona Man had killed? Though one skull was used to anchor an early house, no others have been found. What did the hunters do with over seventy-five others they had collected? Last, in one small hut at

Terra Amata lay the remains of an ancient wooden bowl. Near it were lumps of red ochre or hematite, pointed like pencils at one end. Around the world primitive man has used this porous red material to draw ceremonial designs on his equipment, on his walls, and on himself.

Had *Homo erectus* begun to venerate the elephant by decorating elephant skulls with red ochre? Had he begun to stage midnight ceremonies in sacred places—still undiscovered—where he left the skulls behind? Had he begun to whittle amulets to bring success to his hunts? If so, he had begun to believe that the forces of nature existed as "beings"; that they could be propitiated, coerced, and venerated in order to bring him luck.

The most widespread and ancient of all human religious beliefs is thought to be animism. This is the belief that trees, rocks, plants, animals, stars, wind, sun, rain—all the animate and inanimate "beings" of the universe—have souls; if human life is to be maintained, these souls or beings must be recognized and propitiated in some fashion.

Curiously, Jane Goodall observed what looked like the very beginnings of animism among her chimps at Gombe. On a gray overcast morning at the beginning of the wet season she was casually recording a group of chimps feeding in a fig tree. As the rains began, heavy drops pelted the leaves, the chimps, and Jane. She expected the chimps to sit, hunch their shoulders, and miserably endure the storm. But what she witnessed next, neither she nor any other thinking evolutionist will soon forget.

When the rains began in earnest, the chimps—over fifteen individuals in all—climbed down from the fig tree and began to plod up the steep, grassy slope toward an open, barren ridge. The females scrambled into trees near the top of the ridge while the males hunkered on the exposed peaks. Suddenly the sky opened up, the rains intensified, and a shocking clap of thunder stunned every hearing creature in the valley.

As if the moment had finally come, one large male chimp stood upright, swayed rhythmically from foot to foot, and screamed. Then he charged headlong off the ridge and down the slope. Soon another rose, howled at the storm, and barreled off the ridge. Then another and another followed. Some broke off tree branches as they ran, then stopped to shake them at the sky and hurl them to the ground. Others dragged branches behind them and then beat the branches against the trees as they galloped by.

Goodall sat, astonished, unable even to open her recording book. She thought this would be the end of the display. But as the last male hollered at the heavens, then charged the earth, the first of the performers began to reascend the slope toward the ridge. The others followed, and for the next twenty minutes Goodall watched seven adult male chimpanzees ascend the ridge, stand up on their hind legs, shake their fists or branches, scream at the thunder, lightning, and pounding rain, then charge down the slippery slope, hurling branches as they went. During the next ten years of study Goodall saw this communal "rain dance" occur only two other times.

Did man first begin to confront the forces of nature like this—with dances and antics to vent his frustration? And what if, in the middle of one of these primitive performances, the rain subsided and the sun broke through the clouds? If these coincidences occurred several times, would not primitive man have begun to believe that the forces of nature existed as supernatural beings, that man's primitive rituals could actually influence them?

Moreover, as their brains evolved, would not *Homo erectus* people have begun to stage more elaborate performances, dances to bring the elephants, ceremonies to make the berries grow big and fat, rituals to make the fig trees bloom prodigiously? And wouldn't these performances have begun to be directed at the very object of their concern? If they wanted to hunt elephants, wouldn't they direct their ceremonies toward the life power of the elephant? If they wanted figs or berries, wouldn't they direct their ceremonies toward the life force of the fig trees or the berry patch? This way primitive man began to see that everything around him was imbued with life; that—if he performed ceremonies to venerate these life forces—he could influence his own destiny.

But *Homo erectus* did not always have time to dance, hoot, and holler in order to propitiate the life forces of the wind, the elephants, the birds, or the berry patches. So perhaps individuals began to carry "special" stones, "special" whittled sticks, "sacred" pieces of bone, and other things as amulets—magic bits of their environment that expressed recognition and reverence for supernatural beings. Certainly the missing elephant skulls and whittled wood at Torralba, and the pencil-sharp chunks of red ochre at Terra Amata suggest that by half a million years ago *Homo erectus* had begun to stage ceremonies, to decorate himself with red paint and amulets, to recognize and propitiate the "supernatural."

Most provocative of all about these European sites is that no human skeletons have been found. Surely someone must have died during one of the dangerous hunting escapades staged at Torralba and Ambrona. Certainly some infant, old person, or injured adolescent must have passed away in one of the oval huts at Terra Amata? Where are their remains?

Elephants are the only animals that bury their dead. They are intelligent creatures who, despite their huge size, can quickly and quietly disappear from trackers. As a result, stories of their burial ceremonies come only from a few astonished people who have, by accident, witnessed them. Among those individuals is Irven Buss, an authority on these gray giants. In 1963 he was engaged in mapping the movement of African elephants. He had decided to tranquilize one member of an elephant group (normally a band of several mature females and their young), plant a radio transmitter in this creature, then follow the bleeps of the transmitter in his bush plane.

It seemed like a good idea. But unfortunately when Buss shot his dart into the side of a young cow, she collapsed. And in forty-five minutes she died—overdosed. At first the other elephants angrily trumpeted and aimlessly shuffled around the stricken cow. But when she died, the oldest female in the group coaxed the others to the edge of a nearby forest. Then she returned alone, broke branches from surrounding trees, pulled up nearby grass, and covered the head and shoulders of her dead relative with this debris.

Burials are not seen among any of the primates except man. In one recent observation of chimps, a group of seventeen individuals, adult males and females, adolescents, and one infant, met at a group of fig and palm trees beside a rocky stream bed in Tanzania. One chimp, Rix, slipped from a tree and fell to his death in the gully below. His neck was broken. The others exploded—screaming, shrieking, crying, and wailing in a manner known only to highly agitated chimps. Many stood upright, staggered from foot to foot, beat the ground with their fists and feet, tore off leaves, hurled sticks or stones, or dashed around the clearing below the trees. Others huddled, whimpering, patting and embracing each other. After several minutes of this melee, which could be heard throughout the valley, the display became sporadic and twelve adults formed a rough circle around the corpse. Except for Godi—the constant companion of the dead chimp—who continued to scream, all sat silently and stared at Rix. But four hours later the last of Rix's friends departed. They left no dirt, no grass, no branches, no special sticks or stones to commemorate their comrade's place of death.

Chimps don't desert their dying friends until the end, however. When an old female at Gombe was attacked by four males from a neighboring group, she escaped to thick underbrush near the trail. She was severely wounded, with deep open cuts and broken bones. Her ten-year-old daughter stayed with her, sweeping the flies from her mother's wounds and holding her hand until she died. Female chimps often hold their dead infants for several days before they drop them in the bushes. But there is no further ceremony.

So what motive would early man have to bury his dead friends or relatives? If man had begun to recognize the stars, the sun, the moon, the rain, the plants and animals around him as "beings," then it seems likely that he had recognized that he too had an essence, a being, a soul. Certainly *Homo erectus* had begun to dream at night, to dream of himself and others as disembodied entities that could take strange leaps in time and place, travel to unknown realms, talk to dead friends and relatives, confront supernatural creatures. Quite likely he had experienced hallucinogenic visions during famine-stricken weeks, visions of other times, other realms. So it would not be difficult for him to imagine that at death his soul could travel, disembodied, to other places. And being an optimist, perhaps he began to bury his dead so that their souls could go to better realms beyond everyday reality. Such a ceremony would also serve to console and unite the relatives of the dead man and to protect the body from scavengers and enemies.

How *erectus* buried his dead was probably first by individual whim which later became tradition within the group. Perhaps, like the elephants, some people began by covering the corpse with leaves and twigs. Maybe they put the body in a sleeping position before they buried it so that it could sleep comfortably—

or be reborn—in the world beyond. Maybe they took the skull of the deceased, ate the brains to acquire the dead man's courage, wisdom, or power, and placed it alone in a sacred, secret graveyard.

No *Homo erectus* graves have been found. But a 60,000-year-old burial site recently discovered in a cave high in the hills above a valley in Iraq gives a clue to *Homo erectus* burial practices. Here Ralph Solecki of Columbia University excavated pollen from around a skeleton that had been laid in a shallow grave. By palynology—the science of recognizing ancient plants from fossil pollens—it was discovered that people had gathered ancestral versions of grape hyacinths, bachelor's buttons, hollyhocks, and yellow-flowering groundsel in the valley and carefully placed them on the grave. Perhaps *Homo erectus* had begun this funeral rite thousands of years before.

Such great social thinkers as Edward Tylor, Sir James Frazer, Emile Durkheim, and many others disagree about the origin of religion. Some say the belief in one's personal soul—generated through dreams and visions—preceded the belief in animism or recognition of other realms and supernatural beings. Some say magic preceded religion of any sort. In the literature they argue about when man began to distinguish between ordinary and supernatural phenomena, when fetishism—the worship of material objects supposed to have inherent power—was first used, when man began to worship his ancestors, when he began to see God as the creator, when he first associated the concept of morality on earth with rewards in the afterlife.

No one knows. But the missing elephant skulls and missing human skeletons at early European sites suggest that the roots of religious belief were firmly planted a half million years ago. Such belief could finally explain why the plants had not bloomed or the elephants not come by that year, why the sun disappeared every evening, why the stars circled the earth, where man had come from and where he was going after death. Religion was man's first attempt to explain nature and his place in it. Some day his curiosity would drive him to look for new explanations—scientific ones.

Religion did something else for early man, however, something perhaps far more important than explaining nature. As Durkheim points out in his 1912 book *The Elementary Forms of the*

Religious Life, religion brought individuals together. It united them through mutual ceremonies, rituals, and beliefs.

So, perhaps, did shamanism—the oldest living medical tradition. Shamans are intermediaries, members of the community who—by trance, by dance, by chants, by personal sacrifice and visions—are able to enter the world of the supernatural. Here they are thought to gain knowledge, capture power, and enlist the help of supernatural forces. These resources they use during shamanic ceremonies to cure the illnesses of their friends and relatives.

Today shamanism is practiced by people from the tundras of Siberia to the jungles of the Amazon; and though oceans, mountains, and deserts have isolated these peoples for thousands of years, around the world their shamanic methods are remarkably similar. Perhaps because they work.

Michael Harner, an anthropologist at the New School for Social Research, spent many years with the Jívaro Indians of the forested eastern slopes of the Ecuadorian Andes. Among them he learned their ancient art of shamanism. Since then he has worked with shamans of several North American Indian tribes, and he himself has become a seer, or shaman. As anthropologist and shaman he became so impressed with the effectiveness of these healing techniques that he wrote a book describing some shamanic practices, and he has begun to teach the shamanic way to students in America and Europe. Curiously, Harner finds that students of all creeds ". . . easily become initiated into the fundamentals of shamanic practice." Perhaps, as he says, because "the ancient way is so powerful, and taps so deeply into the human mind, that one's usual cultural belief systems and assumptions about reality are essentially irrelevant." From Harner's pioneering work—and results—it appears that shamanism is deeply engraved in the human mind.

Why shamanism produces effective cures is unknown—though fascinating theories are emerging. Perhaps the shamanic trance, induced by the shaman and transferred to his patient, triggers natural opiates (endorphins) in the brain to relieve pain. This trance state may also trigger the body's natural immune system (which is also housed in the brain) to begin the healing process. Harner has just begun to explore the possibilities.

When and how shamans first developed their ancient skills is, of course, also unknown. But a final look at chimps may give a clue. Though Jane Goodall saw the "rain dance" performed as a group ceremony only a handful of times, she often saw older chimps stage individual dances at the start of heavy rains. At the beginning of one deluge, she reports, Flo's son Figan swung wildly in the tree above his mother, leaping from limb to limb, flinging leaves and branches, kicking his legs, swinging his arms, and screaming at the sky.

Was Figan smart enough to begin to think that he personally could commune with nature, control it, harness its impetuous, unpredictable whims? Probably not. But by the time of *Homo erectus*, when our ancestors had developed larger brains, had begun to bury their dead, to believe in their souls and in the souls of the plants and animals around them, to recognize other realms and supernatural beings, surely some from among them, like Figan, must have begun to experiment with private communication. Several techniques were dropped as useless. Others seemed to work. And gradually *Homo erectus* men and women learned to employ trances, to "travel" to netherworlds, to harness energy, and to enlist this power to help their friends.

Homo erectus probably didn't engage in shamanic ceremonies every day, however. As practiced around the world today, these are often long events, lasting several hours or even days. They normally involve the whole community and are performed only when someone is seriously sick of some unknown cause. So, for more minor ailments like broken bones, colds, coughs, burns, and flesh wounds, *Homo erectus* probably used other remedies. Bones were set or left to heal themselves. Ointments, salves, and poultices were applied to burns and wounds. Saunas and steambaths may have been used for aching muscles, stiff necks, pulled ligaments, and pinched nerves. And herbal drinks were probably the time-honored remedies for upset stomachs, colds, and coughs. Through trial and error they discovered those that worked and gradually pharmacology began.

Other things were evolving too. Since groups of *Homo erectus* people were staging massive, cooperative elephant kills and living contentedly in clusters of houses, their system of rights and obligations must have grown dramatically more complex. Women who shared a fire were obliged to share food. Men who lived together hunted together and were bound by duty to divide the spoils in specific ways. Certain categories of relatives and friends were expected to do favors for you, others to joke with you, some to advise you, some to exchange gifts with you, some to trade secrets with you.

These customs of reciprocity had to be maintained. Liars, cheaters, and lazy individuals had to be reformed. Someone, or some ones, had to organize public activities and make decisions on behalf of the whole community. So *Homo erectus* must have needed a framework of authority, a system of leaders and followers, some general rules of law and order, some simple methods to support the network of rights and obligations, some means of punishing offenders. In short, some simple form of government.

If one can accept the definition of government proposed by the English anthropologist Radcliffe-Brown as ". . . that part of the total organization of a society which is concerned with the maintenance or establishment of social order by the organized exercise of coercive authority," then its roots began long before *Homo erectus*. All social, group-living primates have hierarchies, pecking orders, and the most powerful animal, the smartest animal, the most ambitious animal, the animal best able to get attention, the animal most clever at enlisting the support of others, becomes the leader. And animals are not beyond making clever political maneuvers to become "top dog." When Goodall's chimp Figan wanted to overthrow Humphrey, the dominant male animal of the Gombe troop, he simply enlisted his brother's help. When Figan was alone with Humphrey, he was aggressive. But only when his brother Faben appeared did he actually make a display of strength. After several of these strategic moves, Humphrey was subdued and Figan assumed leadership of the group. Among the primates, hierarchies establish social order, individuals maintain that social order by defending their position (or establishing a new one), and leaders lead the group.

But our primate relatives have no complicated system of rights and obligations to each other. They never share their vegetables and only begrudgingly share meat. They are not "obliged" to do favors for one another, to follow the leader, to cooperate in a hunt, to divide the spoils "fairly." They deal with their peers and establish their positions with wits, guts, charm, and strength. Certainly no sophisticated rules of reciprocity dominate their lives.

Homo erectus people, however, had acquired social debts. And to protect this system of reciprocity—upon which all individuals had become dependent for survival—they must have ventured far from primate hierarchies to a more elaborate form of maintaining social order.

It probably began quite simply. Perhaps at first the strongest, most charismatic, most politically clever individual led the group. And simple gossip—that infernal compulsion so deeply ingrained in the human species that no man or woman has not indulged in it—probably established social norms, aired public opinion, and curbed petty crime. Other early means of social control were ridicule, humiliation, avoidance, denial of favors, and refusal to recognize obligations.

More complicated government probably began when *Homo erectus* individuals started to gather around the evening fire to talk. At these primitive assembly meetings, plans were made, problems were discussed, grievances were heard, customs were recognized, rules were established. Undoubtedly they decided that criminals had to be punished or persuaded to make restitution to the injured party. Perhaps they established the ancient rule of "an eye for an eye, a tooth for a tooth." So a murderer was killed, or one of his relatives was killed in place of him. Maybe they chose to ostracize the murderer instead. For lesser crimes the offender might have paid a fine in meat, vegetables, tools, or extra work.

In some areas these assemblies may have been dominated by one powerful person, in others by a group of respected elders. Perhaps an age group of young men or women, or both, led the discussion. Probably a decision was made by mutual agreement of all attending group members. Then the rules were implemented by force in numbers. In this way government began, and with it politics—all the ploys that individuals or groups of individuals use to influence others or to maintain or advance their position in the social network.

Intricately involved with the evolution of religion and government was the concept of "us" and "them." Even this probably started long before *Homo erectus* times. All animals know who are friends and who are not. Dogs know which other dogs live in their neighborhood and which are strangers. So do fish, birds, elephants, bears, and all the primates. Baboons know when a strange male appears and lingers at the edge of the troop. Gorillas know when an uninvited male enters the harem. Chimpanzees recognize their mothers, siblings, friends, and enemies. All these creatures know who will help them in a fight and who will join the other side. The concept of "us" and "them" is deeply engraved in every living social species.

So it is with human beings. In fact, in many places today, people see outsiders as not quite human. The Yanamamo of Venezuela call all other people "Naba," or "near human." The word Zuni, the name by which these Indians of the American Southwest call themselves, means "we, the real people." Americans use derogatory slang terms for immigrants and outsiders. So do the Europeans and Asians. Almost uniformly, people have a word for "us" and a word or words for "them."

Although at first our ancestors might have lacked words for "us" and "them", they must have distinguished these categories: When the protohominids had started to bond over 4 million years ago, individuals must have begun to see themselves as members of a family and a band. This was "us." Because families and bands congregated with others seasonally at particular lakes, streams, berry patches, and fruiting trees, and because these groups exchanged mates, traded favors, and recognized certain rights and obligations to one another, this larger group was also considered "us." "Them" was everybody else—everyone they didn't know and didn't marry, all the strangers with whom no rights and obligations were shared.

How they got along with "them" probably varied. It is unlikely that early men and women spent much time defending their entire range. No one had time. Besides, they didn't need to, because they moved from place to place and there was often enough room for everyone. But undoubtedly they had skirmishes if strangers usurped camping, gathering, and hunting spots where they went regularly.

This is normal in the animal world. Most animals (or groups of animals) defend the territory they think is theirs, do battle with intruders, and sometimes invade surrounding territories to extend their realm. Among the higher primates, the gibbons, our Southeast Asian arboreal relatives, line up at the border of their territory and scream at their unfriendly neighbors to establish a boundary. Male orangs charge intruders who wander into their territory. And as mentioned earlier, chimpanzees stage raids in which a group of males range far into the territory of their neighbors, killing chimpanzee enemies—including females and children—and stealing their lands.

Our ancestors probably did the same. They defended what they needed in order to survive, fled when they were outnumbered, and stole other people's important places when they could. *Homo erectus* bands certainly had had a fight at Choukoutien. They must have attempted to secure their right to kill elephants at Torralba and Ambrona and to build their houses at Terra Amata. Whether they defended these places year-round seems unlikely, but surely they must have tried to drive away strangers whom they encountered. So, if they saw intruders at their waterholes, in their caves, at their hunting sites or nut groves, they probably lined up along a border and hurled insults, sticks, and stones. If their enemies actually succeeded in taking over their regular places, they probably attempted to ambush the intruders, kill them while they slept, raid their supplies, or engage in hand-to-hand combat to drive them out. Sometimes they probably also tried to negotiate with "them."

But what was life really like in the times of *Homo erectus* people 500,000 years ago? The only thing we know for certain is that they were nomads who moved from place to place, hunting when the time was right, gathering when it wasn't. For years anthropologists have been downgrading this nomadic hunting/gathering existence as "laborious," as an "incessant quest for food," as "eking out a bare existence in an environment of unreliable resources." The phrases have become clichés. As one well-respected archaeologist put it: "A man who spends his whole life following animals just to kill them to eat, or moving from one berry patch to another, is really living just like an animal himself."

Not so, says anthropologist Marshall Sahlins. He examined statistics taken from many traditional hunting/gathering societies, among them the Kung Bushmen of the rugged Kalahari Desert of southern Africa. Before Western influence changed daily life, Kung men hunted from two to two and a half days a week, with an average workweek of fifteen hours. Women gathered for about the same period of time each week. In fact, one day's work supplied her family with vegetables for the next three days. Throughout the year both men and women worked for a couple of days, then took a couple off to rest, play games, gossip, plan rituals, and visit. Moreover, their food was both varied and abundant—so abundant that often hundreds of their favorite nuts lay around them rotting on the ground. Even their dogs ate well. So it seems the Bushmen worked less, had more leisure time, ate well, and got much more rest than we do.

Apparently other aboriginals had a lot of leisure time too. For example, one 1840s squatter in the Australian outback wondered ". . . how that sage people managed to pass their time before my party came and taught them to smoke." This reaction was similar to that of a traveler among the Micmac Indians of Quebec, Canada. In 1616 he reported that ". . . their days are all nothing but pastime." The most remarkable, however, were the traditional Hadza of East Africa. Though their environment looked desolate, they hunted and gathered only a few hours a week, rarely did it in a group, and often ate alone where their prey fell. They had no identifiable form of government and few rules and regulations. They passed their time gambling.

It would appear that the workweek in the old days beats today's banker's hours by quite a bit. Barring unusual circumstances, *Homo erectus* people probably spent a good deal of time relaxing. Everyone worked a while, then napped, chatted, played games, ate, sang, danced, performed religious ceremonies, held feasts and marriage celebrations, and visited their friends. Undoubtedly they also spent time solving disputes, having feuds, doing combat, and traveling from one place to another. Then they worked again. Sahlins is so sure that the ancient hunting/gathering life was leisurely, however, that he concludes: ". . . in fact, this was, when you come to examine it, the original affluent society."

Homo erectus peoples were not, it seems, living like animals. They had migrated out of Africa (though many remained behind) and spread across Eurasia in small groups. Certainly they were moving from hunting snare to berry patch. But they knew which were theirs, which they shared with others, and who didn't belong on the hillsides and bluffs, at the streams and swamps, in the caves or on the grasslands that they roamed. They had learned to control fire, to stage massive hunts on big-game animals, and to build and live in houses. Undoubtedly in the northern regions they had learned to make clothes to endure the freezing weather, and everywhere they made and used an array of beautifully fashioned tools. By inference, it seems they also engaged in primitive religious ceremonies, funeral rituals, healing rites, and council meetings. And with their leisure time they would soon develop a far more complicated culture.

By 20,000 years ago our ancestors had spread to Alaska, into the Americas and remote sections of Australia. Moreover, they had lost the last of their primitive physical characteristics. Their bodies and minds were those of modern man, *Homo sapiens.*

They had started to paint beautiful pictures of animals in caves, to carve small figurines of animals and women from mammoth ivory, to draw and engrave images on the rocks around them. Dots and parallel lines found on bone fragments suggest they may have begun to mark the phases of the moon to record calendrical events. They had begun to bury their dead in elaborate graves with ornaments and tools of the deceased. They were making finely crafted tools and weapons of immense variety in size, shape, and function, along with cordage, netting, matting, and finely cut leather garments. Man had begun to perfect his arts, his knowledge of nature, his religious practices, and his technology.

By 10,000 years ago, in some areas *Homo sapiens* was beginning to grow his own grains, to domesticate some of the animals he hunted, and to settle down. With this would come surplus food, increased population, specialization of crafts, the first pottery, widespread trade, markets, and money of all kinds. Where necessary, more complicated, hierarchial governments evolved to handle the growing population, to distribute property, to control the rights to fuel and water, and to enforce the proliferating body of laws. Now greater differentiation in rank and role, more sophisticated political maneuvers, and more extensive warfare would evolve.

But have we really changed since *Homo erectus* times? We still cross our fingers for good luck, carry amulets and charms, decorate ourselves with paints, wear clothes to suit the fashion of the times. We still play, dance, chant, and sing. We still mutter prayers to unknown forces, perform religious ceremonies, believe in afterworlds, and bury our dead. We still have families, relatives, and friends. We still recognize obligations and exchange gifts—in some places, even spouses.

We still follow social rules and laws, customs and traditions. We even punish criminals the same old way, with fines for petty crimes, with ostracism in the form of jails and—occasionally— with death in the form of capital punishment. We are still bickering over who owns what, and where our boundaries lie. And as ridiculous as it seems, we are still lining up at borders, hurling missiles, and invading other people's lands, murdering and pillaging "them."

Some things seem to have improved. We have conquered smallpox, curtailed polio and many infant and childhood diseases. We have increased the human life-span. We have walked the moon and filled the world with music, art, literature, and sports. Other things seem to have gotten worse. We have less leisure time. Our governments have probably become less democratic. We have had two world wars. Our problem of world hunger has definitely gotten worse. Women—half the human population—have largely lost their ancient status. Crime runs rampant in our cities. And we are overpopulating and polluting our world. Of course times have changed. But in many respects we are still the creatures we were 500,000 years ago.

What about the sex contract, though: Has it changed?

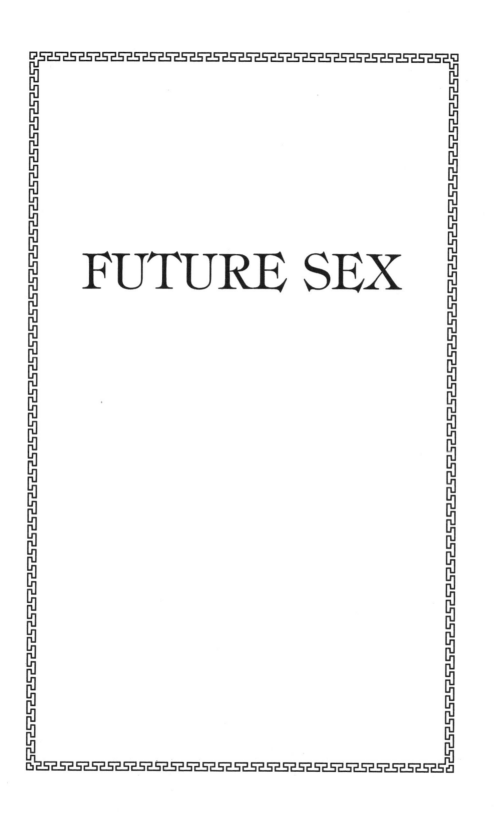

FUTURE SEX

Thus the sum of things is ever being replenished,
and mortals live one and all by give and take.
Some races wax and others wane, and in a short space
the tribes of living things are changed, and
like runners hand on the torch of life.

—LUCRETIUS
De Rerum Natura

If a reporter stopped you on the street, thrust a microphone to your lips and asked, "What is man?" how would you define this animal *Homo sapiens?* A creature who walks on two feet instead of four? A mammal with small canine teeth? A species that returns to a home base every night, hunts meat, and shares his food? Perhaps a creature who recognizes relatives and doesn't mate with kin, or an animal with a big brain who speaks with human language?

No doubt some people would skip over these rather academic distinctions and shoot straight for what is most unusual about us—all the things we make and leave behind. No other creature, not even the chimpanzee and the gorilla, who have I.Q.'s quite close to ours, has left an archaeological record—the remains of culture.

But what if the reporter asked an "informed" chimpanzee the same question: "What is man?" As anthropologist Sherwood Washburn once remarked at a convention, a chimpanzee might respond quite differently. He might single out our ability to make love regularly and our curious habit of bonding with our consorts. This is indeed a distinctive human characteristic—as I maintain, the spark that ignited the history of humanity.

Of course, it wasn't the first thing that happened. Evolution is a mosaic process, the motion of myriad forces in which one change triggers another, which triggers a third, and so on. First came the drop in world temperature, which began by 14 million years ago. That reduced the forests of Africa and Eurasia and forced our earliest relatives, the protohominids, out of the trees and into the woodlands. At this time, females still had a period of heat and the sexes did not bond.

As the earth continued to cool, the woodlands diminished and the grassy boulevards between the woodland trees expanded into plains. So by 10 million years ago, with each new dry season small groups of protohominids were driven onto these savannahs. Here, where group solidarity became essential for protection, our ancestors began to forage within eyesight of each other and to carry their meals to a central place where they could eat unmolested by predators.

But to carry they had to walk. And with selection for efficient walking, perhaps by 10 million years ago, the pelvis began to take its human shape. As a result, the diameter of the pelvic inlet shrank; the female's birth canal got smaller; gradually females began to have difficulty delivering their young. Probably many died. Yet among them were a few females with the genetic proclivity to bear their young in a more immature state. The infants of these mothers easily slipped through the birth canal, survived parturition, and disproportionately lived to adulthood—thus passing on the genetic "instructions" for premature delivery to the female protohominid population.

With this change, the amount of time required to feed and protect infants increased. Moreover, because mothers walked they had to carry their young in their arms instead of on their backs. Now females found it increasingly difficult to keep up with the daytime jaunt, to chase after small animals and join small hunting parties. Motherhood had become a grind. Females needed males to help them raise their children.

But how to enlist male service? Some ancient females were sexier than others. They copulated throughout *more* of their monthly cycle, throughout *more* of their pregnancy, and *sooner* after delivering their young. These females, though burdened down with helpless young, attracted constant and close attention while they were in heat. During daytime expeditions they were in the center of the group. At night, when everyone assembled to beg for meat, these females got the most. Thus sexy females were healthier and safer; their children were healthier and safer too. Therefore the children of sexy females disproportionately lived to adulthood and passed on the genetic propensity to copulate *throughout* the month, *during* pregnancy, and *shortly after* parturition. Protohominid females lost their period of heat.

Finally, because females could copulate shortly after parturition, they acquired the ability to conceive another child directly after delivering one. They began to bear children *more frequently.* Now, instead of coping with only one infant, they sometimes had two or three to care for and they needed *more* help from men. So those females with a slight ability to sustain a bonding relationship—by exchanging sex and vegetables for meat and protection—lived. Gradually, selection bred for females and males with the propensity to bond.

This way the sex contract evolved between primitive men and women more than 4 million years ago. It was a contract cemented by regular sex and designed to help the female raise her young. This bond was not necessarily monogamous. Perhaps a few males were able to support more than one female, and sexy females bonded with more than one male. Due to economic feasibility, however, most individuals probably bonded with only one mate. Nor was this bond necessarily permanent. Perhaps for some individuals it lasted several years or even a lifetime. For most couples, pairing may have lasted only long enough to enable a female to feed and protect her young through infancy.

But bonding did much more than help the young survive. With time it would initiate such primal human emotions as jealousy and altruism, the human drive to categorize people in terms of kin, the human ability to communicate by sophisticated language, the human capacity for complicated thought, the human need to make tools, weapons, houses, governments, rules, enemies, gods, and afterworlds.

Modern sociologists have applied a lot of ink to paper, fretting over the state of the human family. They ask: "Will it survive?" As one scientist expressed it in *Science* magazine: "At the present accelerating rate of depletion, the United States will run out of families not long after it runs out of oil."

Scientists and laymen alike note with discomfort the flagrant promiscuity, adultery, and rape seen in industrial societies today, the new methods of birth control, legalized abortion, the incidence of family violence, the frequency of incest, the amount of illegitimacy, the percentage of couples "living together," the homosexuals emerging from the closet, the experimental free-sex colonies, the anything-goes spas and nightclubs, the high divorce rate, the single-parent families, the "New Morality."

Is the family an endangered species? I think not. Promiscuity and adultery are found in every society ever studied—probably because we are naturally promiscuous, as are our ape relatives. Rape is common in many species, including our close cousins the orangutans, and it is committed in all human cultures. It is particularly prevalent among the Eskimos and South American Indians. In fact, among some Brazilian tribes, gang rape is a legitimate means of punishing promiscuous women.

Abortion and infanticide, the *original* forms of birth control, have been legally practiced in societies around the world for hundreds of years. Within-family violence is a normal occurrence in every culture studied—and many of the fights have to do with sex. Among the Bushmen, for example, more than half of all family arguments resulted from sexual jealousy.

Although the amount of incest seems high today, Sigmund Freud remarked on its incredible frequency among his patients in 1897, and Suetonius wrote of its astonishing prevalence among the upper echelons of Roman society in the declining years of the Roman empire.

That today's young adults are "living together" before marriage is not a new invention—in many traditional cultures this has been sanctioned (even encouraged) for centuries. Homosexuality was common in ancient Greece, as it is today in societies from New Guinea to the Netherlands. Free-sex colonies aren't new either—they were experimented with in nineteenth-century America and were popular in early eighteenth-century western Europe.

Orgies, mate-swapping, illicit love affairs, adultery, rape, abortion, incest, "living together," and homosexuality have been going on for thousands if not millions of years. And none of this has endangered the status of the family. Nor are these sexual patterns likely to change dramatically. As long as females are continually sexually receptive—which undoubtedly will be for the duration of our existence as a species—people will continue to experiment with sex.

But bonding is a much more complicated matter than sexual affairs. It is a contract, a commitment made between individuals to accept mutual duties, obligations, and responsibilities. And around the world this contract is still made. In some parts of India a woman ideally marries several men. In the Muslim world men hope to marry several women. In most societies, we marry one. But everywhere on earth people are still bonding.

Perhaps the custom of monogamy will change. As Robin Fox says: "Left to their own devices, societies will work out some form of multiple mating system. Monogamy has never worked." Indeed, this change has already begun. Most Westerners are not by-and-large monogamous. We practice "serial monogamy," bonding first with one mate, breaking up, and bonding with another. So do people in all other societies. Divorce is permitted everywhere. Yet most individuals around the world who do divorce will proceed to bond again.

The most frequently cited threat to bonding is today's increasing number of single-parent families. These are seen predominantly in Western urban settings where a single parent *can* economically raise a child or children alone. Female chimpanzees, gorillas, and orangutans raise their young alone and, where possible, some human females will do the same. *Bonding is no longer necessary to keep the young alive.* Yet, unlike our ape relatives, most single mothers initially bonded to produce their young, remained with their mate until their children passed through infancy, and broke their bond to find a new mate or mates more to their liking. And, curiously, 13 percent of American single-parent families are run by fathers—a role rarely adopted by other primate males.

Bonding is deeply engraved in the human psyche. Teenagers "naturally" experiment at bonding and young adults around the world strive to bond to raise their young. The drive to bond is so strong that we even bond with no intention of producing children. Homosexuals often bond with their lovers. Couples who "live together" bond. Older people bond long after their reproductive years are over. Interestingly, these bonds are hard to break. Teenage bonds often linger into adulthood, long after the purpose of the bond has become defunct. Married people normally remain with their mates several years after they have lost interest in them. Divorced couples often continue to argue the same old way or try to establish a permanent friendship bond.

Bonding is like other behavior patterns man acquired from his past. From living in the trees we acquired a fear of falling. We still dream of falling and many of us have an irrational fear of heights. Many of us also fear closed places, and almost all children are afraid of the dark and fearful of being left alone.

We still drop litter as if we were in the trees. We still greet each other the way the apes do, with handshakes, pats, kisses, and hugs. We still gesture, posture, and grimace to make our feelings known. We still crave sweets, take midday naps, and groom our friends when we see a bit of lint on another's collar. We still tickle, chase, and copy one another. When one person cries, or laughs, or eats too fast, those around him often do the same. And in every congregation of people—large or small—there is a pecking order. These behavior patterns are part of our primate heritage and they show no signs of changing.

Upon this primate pattern man developed bonding—and with it all the basic human emotions that kept bonds intact. Like our other primitive fears and habits, these emotions have not been shed. We still flirt. We still feel infatuation at the beginning of our bond, allegiance during it, and often sorrow when it is over. We feel guilty when we are promiscuous, jealous or vengeful when our bond is sexually betrayed. Men still worry about being cuckolded. Women still worry about being deserted. We don't need these emotions in our industrial world. We don't need to bond—yet we continue to do it.

To bond is human. It began long ago with the sex contract, and though the rules of the contract will change with changing times, the instinct to make a contract will prevail.

APPENDIX A
TRAJECTORY OF HUMAN EVOLUTION

STAGE/TRAITS	ENVIRONMENT	MILLIONS OF YEARS AGO*
<u>Dryopithecus</u>	forest	20

Living and sleeping in
   trees
Swinging through trees,
   quadrupedal on the
   ground
Centrifugal groups (15 to
   45 individuals) that
   congregate when food is
   abundant
Staple: soft fruits
Supplement: insects,
   grubs, worms, lizards,
   etc.
Estrous periodicity; pro-
   miscuous mating; con-
   sorts
Animal call system
Territory of core areas defined, occasionally defended

<u>Protohominid A</u>	forest fringe; woodlands	10

Living on the ground by
   day, in the trees at
   night

*Stages and times are arbitrary and used for clarification only.

STAGE/TRAITS	ENVIRONMENT	MILLIONS OF YEARS AGO
Quadrupedal traveling; standing		
Evolved teeth for chewing hard foods		
Gathering staple: tough fruits		
Scavenging and catching supplement: small mammals, lizards, turtles, eggs, nestling birds, etc.		
Incipient sharing of meat		
No sharing of vegetables		
Centripetal matricentric groups (5 to 15 individuals) in dry season		
Larger, centrifugal rainy-season groups		
Incipient tool use: digging stick and stones used but not carried		
Incipient weapon use: sticks, stones, and bones used but not carried		
Estrous periodicity; promiscuous mating; consorts		
Protohominid B	woodlands; savannah	9
Centripetal matricentric groups		
Bipedal walking		

Carrying of food, tools,
  weapons
Home bases on the
  ground

<u>Protohominid C</u> "Hoot"   savannah;   8
                                      woodlands

Reduction of pelvic inlet
Selection for premature
  parturition
Burdens of child care in-
  creasing for females
SELECTION FOR: loss of
  estrous periodicity
  copulation during preg-
    nancy
  copulation soon after
    parturition
  ovulation soon after
    parturition
RESULT:
Increased female fertility
Females overburdened
  with *more* premature
  births
Extended consorts, incip-
  ient bonding
Male/female sharing and
  division of labor
Sexual selection for male/
  female secondary sexual
  characteristics
Incorporation of male into
  nuclear family/matri-
  centric extended family
Selection for individuals
  with tendency to bond

STAGE/TRAITS	ENVIRONMENT	MILLIONS OF YEARS AGO
<u>Hominid A</u> "Lucy"	savannah; woodlands	4
Centripetal extended families Nuclear families in dry season Bonding Serial monogamy Evolution of the social emotions Incipient kinship and language		
<u>Hominid B</u>	savannah; woodlands	2
Expansion and reorganization of brain Tool making, weapon making Constructing lean-tos Incipient "big game" hunting Advanced sharing and cooperation		
<u>Homo</u> "Fleet"	savannah; woodlands; tundra	1
Migration from Africa Fire, clothing, houses "Big game" hunting		

Advanced tool making
and weapon making
Advanced kinship, lan-
guage
Incipient religion, government, politics, tribalism

APPENDIX B
MAN'S FAMILY TREE

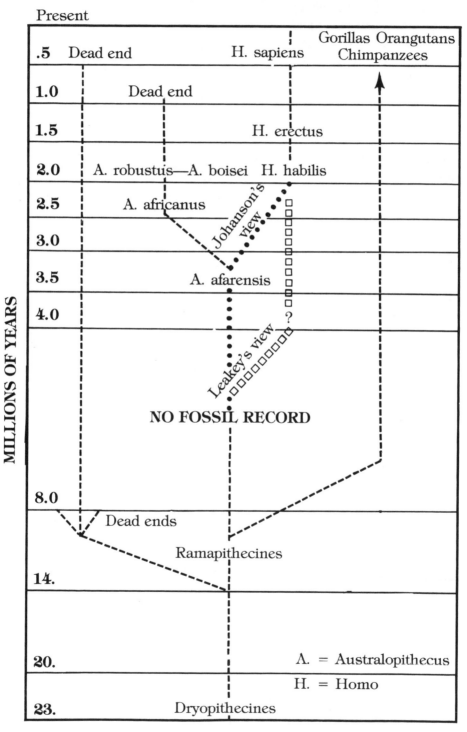

Our family tree has been drawn dozens of ways. This one represents the most recent anthropological views and the present argument between Don Johanson and Richard Leakey.

Sarich and Wilson feel the apes diverged from a common ancestral stock as recently as 6 million years ago, and they cite their biochemical analysis of primate blood proteins. Though there is no fossil record to prove it, many other anthropologists think that the ancestors of the chimpanzees, gorillas, and orangutans diverged from the basal Dryopithecine stock by several million years before Sarich and Wilson's date.

Other early species were forced into the woodlands and savannahs shortly after 14 million years ago. Several proliferated and died, leaving no trace of themselves by 8 million years ago. The most recently extinct was a colossal ape that roamed the grasslands of Eurasia until half a million years ago.

It is generally believed that the Ramapithecines (protohominids) were the first of the human line. *A. africanus*, *A. robustus*, and *A. boisei*, once considered the next members of our lineage, are today believed to be an extinct sideline that ran parallel to that of early *Homo*.

Present controversy surrounds the placement of *A. afarensis*. Don Johanson and his colleagues (represented by dots) think *A. afarensis* is in our lineage. Richard Leakey and others (represented by squares) do not. They believe that the Ramapithecines led to an early *Homo* form about 6 million years ago and that someday the fossils will be discovered to prove it.

BIBLIOGRAPHY

Altman, Jeanne, Stuart A. Altman, and Glenn Hausfater. "Primate Infants' Effects on Mother's Future Reproduction." *Science,* Vol. 201 (Sept. 15, 1978).

Andrews, Peter, and Judith A. H. Van Couvering. "Paleoenvironments in the East African Miocene," in *Approaches to Primate Paleobiology,* ed. Szalay, *Contrib. Primat.,* Vol. 5. Basel: Karger, 1975.

Barash, David P. *Sociobiology and Behavior.* New York: Elsevier, 1977.

Beach, Frank A., ed. *Human Sexuality in Four Perspectives.* Baltimore: Johns Hopkins University Press, 1977.

Berggren, W. A., and C. D. Hollister. "Plate Tectonics and Paleocirculation—Commotion in the Ocean." *Tectonophysics,* Vol. 38 (1977).

Boaz, Noel T. "Early Hominid Population Densities: New Estimates." *Science,* Vol. 206 (Nov. 2, 1979).

Buettner-Janusch, John. *Origins of Man.* New York: John Wiley and Sons, 1967.

Butzer, Karl W. *Environment and Archaeology: An Ecological Approach to Prehistory.* Chicago: Aldine Publishing, 1971.

Calder, Nigel. *The Restless Earth.* New York: Viking Press, 1972.

Campbell, Bernard, ed. *Sexual Selection and the Descent of Man.* Chicago: Aldine Publishing, 1972.

Caplan, Arthur L., ed. *The Sociobiology Debate: Readings on the Ethical and Scientific Issues Concerning Sociobiology.* New York: Harper & Row, 1978.

Chagnon, Napoleon A. *Yanamamö: The Fierce People,* 2nd ed. New York: Holt, Rinehart & Winston, 1977.

Chesters, Kathleen I. M. "The Miocene Flora of Rusinga Island, Lake Victoria, Kenya." *Palaeontographica,* Vol. 101B (1957).

Chevalier-Skolnikoff, Suzanne. "Male-Female, Female-Female, and Male-Male Sexual Behavior in the Stumptail Monkey, with Special Attention to the Female Orgasm." *Archives of Sexual Behavior,* Vol. 3, No. 2 (1974).

————, and Frank E. Poirier. *Primate Bio-Social Development: Biological, Social, and Ecological Determinants.* New York: Garland Publishing, 1977.

Cooke, H. B. S. "Suid Evolution and Correlation of African Hominid Localities: An Alternative Taxonomy." *Science,* Vol. 201 (Aug. 4, 1978).

Darwin, Charles. *The Descent of Man, and Selection in Relation to Sex.* Detroit: Gale Research, 1974.

————. *The Expression of the Emotions in Man and Animals.* Chicago: University of Chicago Press, 1965.

————. *The Origin of Species.* New York: New American Library, 1958.

Dawkins, Richard. *The Selfish Gene.* New York: Oxford University Press, 1976.

DeVore, Irven, ed. *Primate Behavior: Field Studies of Monkeys and Apes.* New York: Holt, Rinehart & Winston, 1965.

Dolhinow, Phyllis. *Primate Patterns.* New York: Holt, Rinehart & Winston, 1972.

Eaton, G. Gray. "The Social Order of Japanese Macaques." *Scientific American* (October 1976).

Eibl-Eibesfeldt, Irenäus. *Ethology: The Biology of Behavior.* New York: Holt, Rinehart & Winston, 1975.

Falk, Dean. "Language, Handedness, and Primate Brains: Did the Australopithecines Sign?" *American Anthropologist,* Vol. 82, No. 1 (March 1980).

Fisher, Helen E. *The Loss of Estrous Periodicity in Hominid Evolution.* Ann Arbor, Mich.: University Microfilms, 1975.

Ford, C. S., and F. A. Beach. *Patterns of Sexual Behavior.* New York: Hoeber, 1951.

Fossey, Dian. "The Imperial Mountain Gorilla." *National Geographic,* Vol. 159, No. 4 (April 1981).

Fox, Robin. *Biosocial Anthropology.* London: Malaby Press, 1975.

————. *Kinship and Marriage.* Middlesex, England: Penguin Books, 1967.

————, and Usher Fleising. "Human Ethology." *Ann. Rev. Anthropol.,* Vol. 5 (1976).

Fried, Morton H. *The Evolution of Political Society.* New York: Random House, 1967.

Galdikas, Biruté M. F. "Living with the Great Orange Apes." *National Geographic,* Vol. 157, No. 6 (June 1980).

Goldin-Meadow, Susan, and Heidi Feldman. "The Development of Language-like Communication without a Language Model." *Science,* Vol. 197 (July 22, 1977).

Goodall, Jane. "Life and Death at Gombe." *National Geographic,* Vol. 155, No. 5 (May 1979).

Goodall, Jane van Lawick. *In the Shadow of Man.* New York: Dell, 1971.

Goss-Custard, J. D., R. I. M. Dunbar, and F. P. G. Aldrich-Blake. "Survival, Mating, and Rearing Strategies in the Evolution of Primate Social Structure." *Folia Primatologica,* Vol. 17, No. 1 (1972).

Gould, Stephen Jay. "The Piltdown Conspiracy." *Natural History,* Vol. 89, No. 8 (August 1980).

———. "Piltdown Revisited." *Natural History,* Vol. 88, No. 3 (March 1979).

Harnad, Stevan R., Horst D. Steklis, and Jane Lancaster, eds. "Origins and Evolution of Language and Speech." *Annals of the New York Academy of Sciences,* Vol. 280 (1976).

Harner, Michael. *The Way of the Shaman: A Guide to Power and Healing.* San Francisco, Harper & Row, 1980.

Harris, Marvin. *The Rise of Anthropological Theory.* New York: Thomas Y. Crowell, 1968.

Hewes, Gordon W. "Food Transport and the Origin of Hominid Bipedalism." *American Anthropologist,* Vol. 63 (1961).

Hinde, R. A. *Biological Bases of Human Social Behavior.* New York: McGraw-Hill, 1974.

Hite, Shere. *The Hite Report: A Nationwide Study of Female Sexuality.* New York: Dell Publishing, 1976.

Hockett, Charles F. "The Origin of Speech." *Scientific American,* Vol. 203 (1960).

———, and Robert Ascher. "The Human Revolution." *American Scientist,* Vol. 52 (1964).

Holden, Constance. "Paul Maclean and the Triune Brain." *Science,* Vol. 204 (June 8, 1979).

Holloway, R. L. "The Casts of Fossil Hominid Brains." *Scientific American* (July 1974).

Isaac, Glynn. "The Food-sharing Behavior of Protohuman Hominids." *Scientific American* (April 1976).

———, and Elizabeth R. McCown. *Perspectives on Human Evolution,* Vol. III, *Human Origins: Louis Leakey and the East African Evidence.* Menlo Park, Cal.: W. A. Benjamin, 1976.

Itani, J., and A. Suzuki. "The Social Unit of Chimpanzees." *Primates,* Vol. 8, No. 4 (1967).

Johanson, Donald C., and Maitland A. Edey. *Lucy: The Beginnings of Humankind.* New York: Simon & Schuster, 1981.

Johanson, D. C. and T. D. White. "A Systematic Assessment of Early African Hominids." *Science,* Vol. 203 (January 26, 1979).

Jolly, Alison. *The Evolution of Primate Behavior.* New York: Macmillan, 1972.

Jolly, C. J. "The Seed-Eaters: A New Model for Hominid Differentiation Based on a Baboon Analogy." *Man,* Vol. 5 (1970).

———. "A Suggested Case of Evolution by Sexual Selection in Primates." *Man,* Vol. 63 (1963).

Jordan, Thomas H. "The Deep Structure of the Continents." *Scientific American,* Vol. 240 (January 1979).

Jukes, Thomas H. "Silent Nucleotide Substitutions and the Molecular Evolutionary Clock." *Science,* Vol. 210 (Nov. 28, 1980).

Katchadourian, Herant A., ed. *Human Sexuality: A Comparative and Developmental Perspective.* Berkeley: University of California Press, 1979.

Kinsey, A. C., et al. *Sexual Behavior of the Human Female.* Philadelphia: Saunders, 1953.

Klein, Richard G. "The Ecology of Early Man in Southern Africa." *Science,* Vol. 197 (July 8, 1977).

Konner, Melvin, and Carol Worthman. "Nursing Frequency, Gonadal Function, and Birth Spacing Among !Kung Hunter-Gatherers." *Science,* Vol. 207 (Feb. 15, 1980).

Kortlandt, A., and M. Kooji. "Protohominid Behavior in Primates." *Symp. Zool. Soc. London,* Vol. 10 (1963).

Kretzoi, Miklós. "New Ramapithecines and *Pliopithecus* from the Lower Pliocene of Rudabánya in North-eastern Hungary." *Nature,* Vol. 257 (Oct. 16, 1975).

Lancaster, Jane B. "Carrying and Sharing in Human Evolution." *Human Nature* (February 1978).

———. *Primate Behavior and the Emergence of Human Culture.* New York: Holt, Rinehart & Winston, 1975.

———, and Phillip Whitten. "Family Matters." *The Sciences* (January 1980).

Leakey, Mary D. "Footprints in the Ashes of Time." *National Geographic* (April 1979).

Leakey, Richard E. *People of the Lake.* Garden City, N.Y.: Anchor Press/Doubleday, 1978.

———, and Roger Lewin. *Origins.* New York: E.P. Dutton, 1977.

Lee, Richard B., and Irven DeVore. *Kalahari Hunter-Gatherers: Studies of the !Kung San and their Neighbors.* Cambridge, Mass.: Harvard University Press, 1976.

Lessa, William. *Ulithi: A Micronesian Design for Living.* New York: Holt, Rinehart & Winston, 1966.

Leutenegger, W. "A Functional Interpretation of the Sacrum of *Australopithecus africanus.*" *South African Journal of Science,* Vol. 73 (1977).

——. "Functional Aspects of Pelvic Morphology in Simian Primates." *J. Hum. Evol.* Vol. 3 (1974).

——. "Maternal-Fetal Weight Relationships in Primates." *Folia Primatologica,* Vol. 20 (1973).

——. "Newborn Size and Pelvic Dimensions of *Australopithecus.*" *Nature,* Vol. 240 (Dec. 29, 1972).

Lorenz, Konrad. *On Aggression.* New York: Bantam Books, 1970.

Lovejoy, C. Owen. "The Origin of Man." *Science,* Vol. 211, No. 4479 (Jan. 23, 1981).

Mair, Lucy. *An Introduction to Social Anthropology,* 2nd Ed. New York: Oxford University Press, 1972.

Marshall, Donald S., and Robert C. Suggs, eds. *Human Sexual Behavior: Variations in the Ethnographic Spectrum.* Englewood Cliffs, N.J.: Prentice-Hall, 1971.

Martin, M. Kay, and Barbara Voorhies. *Female of the Species.* New York: Columbia University Press, 1975.

Masters, William H., and Virginia E. Johnson. *Human Sexual Response.* Boston: Little, Brown, 1966.

Messenger, John C. *Inis Beag: Isle of Ireland.* New York: Holt, Rinehart & Winston, 1969.

Montagu, M. F. "Brains, Genes, Culture, Immaturity, and Gestation," in *Culture: Man's Adaptive Dimension,* ed. Montagu. New York: Oxford University Press, 1968.

Morris, Desmond. *Manwatching.* New York: Harry N. Abrams, 1977.

——. *The Naked Ape.* New York: Dell Publishers, 1967.

——. "Nonverbal Leakage: How You Can Tell If Someone's Lying." *New York* magazine (October 17, 1977).

Moskowitz, Breyne Arlene. "The Acquisition of Language." *Scientific American,* Vol. 239 (November 1978).

Nadler, Ronald D. "Sexual Behavior of Captive Lowland Gorillas." *Archives of Sexual Behavior,* Vol. 5, No. 5 (1976).

——. "Sexual Behavior of Captive Orang-Utans." *Archives of Sexual Behavior,* Vol. 6 (1977).

——. "Sexual Behavior of the Chimpanzee in Relation to the Gorilla and Orang-Utan," in *Progress in Ape Research,* ed. B. H. Bourne. New York: Academic Press, 1977.

——. "Sexual Cyclicity in Captive Lowland Gorillas." *Science,* Vol. 189 (Sept. 5, 1975).

Nishida, T. "The Social Group of Wild Chimpanzees in the Mahali Mountains." *Primates,* Vol. 9 (1968).

Oxnard, C. E. "The Place of the Australopithecines in Human Evolution: Grounds for Doubt?" *Nature,* Vol. 258 (Dec. 4, 1975).

Patterson, Francine G. "Ape Language." *Science,* Vol. 211 (Jan. 2, 1981).

————. "Conversations with a Gorilla." *National Geographic*, Vol. 154, No. 4 (October 1978).

Pfeiffer, John. "Current Research Casts New Light on Human Origins." *Smithsonian*, Vol. 11, No. 3 (June 1980).

————. *The Emergence of Man*, 3rd ed. New York: Harper & Row, 1978.

————. "Full-time Fathers." *Science 80* (November 1980).

Pilbeam, David. *The Ascent of Man*. New York: Macmillan, 1972.

————. "Rearranging Our Family Tree." *Human Nature* (June 1978).

————, et al. "Geology and Palaeontology of Neogene Strata of Pakistan." *Nature*, Vol. 270, (22/29 December 1977).

Premack, David, and Guy Woodruff. "Chimpanzee Problem-Solving: A Test for Comprehension." *Science*, Vol. 202 (Nov. 3, 1978).

Quiatt, Duane D., ed. *Primates on Primates*. Minneapolis: Burgess Publishing, 1972.

Ratliff, Merry. *A Reconstruction of Language Evolution Based on a Gestural Model of Language Origin*. Ann Arbor, Mich.: University Microfilms, 1975.

Rowell, T. E. "Baboon Menstrual Cycles Affected by Social Environments." *J. Reprod. Fert.*, Vol. 21 (1970b).

————. "Female Reproductive Cycles and Social Behavior in Primates," in *Advances in the Study of Behavior*, Vol. 4, eds. Lehrman, et al. New York: Academic Press, 1972.

Sagan, Carl. *The Dragons of Eden*. New York: Random House, 1977.

Sahlins, Marshal. *Stone Age Economics*. Chicago: Aldine Publishing, 1972.

Sarich, V.M. "Molecular Clocks and Hominid Evolution After 12 Years." *Am. Journal Phys. Anthrop.* (February 1980).

————. "The Origin of the Hominids: An Immunological Approach," in *Perspectives on Human Evolution*, Vol. 1, eds. L. S. Washburn and P. C. Jay. New York: Holt, Rinehart & Winston, 1968.

Savage-Rumbaugh, E. Sue, et al. "Reference: The Linguistic Essential." *Science*, Vol. 210 (Nov. 21, 1980).

Sherfey, Mary Jane. *The Nature and Evolution of Female Sexuality*. New York: Vintage Books, 1966.

Simons, E. L. "Ramapithecus." *Scientific American* (May 1977).

————, and D. R. Pilbeam. "Preliminary Revision of the Dryopithecinae (Pongidea, Anthropoidea)." *Folia Primat.* Vol. 3 (1965).

————, and D. R. Pilbeam. "*Ramapithecus* (Hominidae, Hominoidea)," in *Evolution of African Mammals*, eds. Vincent J. Maglio and H.B.S. Cooke. Cambridge, Mass.: Harvard University Press, 1978.

—————, P. Andrews, and D. R. Pilbeam. "Cenozoic Apes," in *Evolution of African Mammals*, eds. Vincent J. Maglio and H. B. S. Cooke. Cambridge, Mass.: Harvard University Press, 1978.

Smith, John Maynard. "The Evolution of Behavior." *Scientific American* (September 1978).

Strum, Shirley C. "Life With the Pumphouse Gang." *National Geographic* (May 1975).

Stross, Brian. *The Origin and Evolution of Language*. Dubuque, Iowa: Wm. C. Brown, 1976.

Symons, Donald. *The Evolution of Human Sexuality*. New York: Oxford University Press, 1979.

Suzuki, A. "An Ecological Study of Chimpanzees Living in a Savannah Woodland." *Primates*, Vol. 10, No. 2 (1969).

Teleki, Geza. "Group Response to the Accidental Death of a Chimpanzee in Gombe National Park, Tanzania." *Folia Primatol.*, Vol. 20 (1973).

—————. "The Omnivorous Chimpanzee." *Scientific American* (January 1973).

—————. *The Predatory Behavior of Wild Chimpanzees*. Lewisburg, Pa.: Bucknell University Press, 1973.

Terrace, H. S. "How Nim Chimpsky Changed My Mind." *Psychology Today* (November 1979).

—————, et al. "Can an Ape Create a Sentence." *Science*, Vol. 206 (Nov. 23, 1979).

Tiger, Lionel, and Robin Fox. *The Imperial Animal*. New York: Dell Publishing, 1971.

Van Couvering, Judith Anne Harris. "Community Evolution and Succession in East Africa during the Late Cenozoic," in *Fossils in the Making: Vertebrate Taphonomy and Paleoecology*, eds. A. Behrensmeyer and A. P. Hill. Chicago: University of Chicago Press, 1980.

—————, and J. A. Miller. "Miocene Stratigraphy and Age Determinations, Rusinga Island, Kenya." *Nature*, Vol. 221, No. 5181 (Feb. 15, 1969).

Wade, Michael J. "Kin Selection: Its Components." *Science*, Vol. 210 (Nov. 7, 1980).

Walker, A. H. N. Hoeck, and L. Perez. "Microwear of Mammalian Teeth as an Indicator of Diet." *Science*, Vol. 201 (Sept. 8, 1978).

Walker, A., and R. E. Leakey. "The Hominids of East Turkana." *Scientific American* (February 1978).

Washburn, S. L. "What We Can't Learn About People from Apes." *Human Nature* (November 1978).

————, and Elizabeth R. McCown. *Perspectives on Human Evolution,* Vol. IV, *Human Evolution: Biosocial Perspectives.* Menlo Park, Ca. Benjamin/Cummings Publishing, 1978.

Washburn, S. L., and Ruth Moore. *Ape Into Human: A Study of Human Evolution,* 2nd ed. Boston: Little, Brown, 1980.

White, Tim D. "Evolutionary Implications of Pliocene Hominid Footprints." *Science,* Vol. 208 (April 11, 1980).

————, and J. M. Harris. "Suid Evolution and Correlation of African Hominid Localities." *Science,* Vol. 198 (Oct. 7, 1977).

Wickler, Wolfgang. *The Sexual Code: The Social Behavior of Animals and Men.* Garden City, N.Y.: Anchor Press/Doubleday, 1973.

Wilson, Edward O. "Academic Vigilantism and the Political Significance of Sociobiology." *BioScience,* Vol. 26, No. 3 (March 1976).

————. *On Human Nature.* Cambridge, Mass.: Harvard University Press, 1978.

————. *Sociobiology: The New Synthesis.* Cambridge, Mass.: The Belknap Press of Harvard University Press, 1975.

Windle, William F. "The Cayo Santiago Primate Colony." *Science,* Vol. 209 (Sept. 26, 1980).

Young, William C., ed. *Sex and Internal Secretions.* Baltimore: Williams and Wilkins, 1961.

INDEX